A Practical Skill Development Guide

THE SKILL ARCHITECT

-75 LIFE SKILLS FOR EVERYONE –VOLUME 1

© Copyright, 2021, Prasad Prakash Tupache

All rights are reserved. No part of this book may be reproduced or transmitted in any form by any means; electronic or mechanical including photography, recording, or any information storage or retrieval system; without the prior written consent of its author.

The opinions/ contents expressed in this book are solely of the author and do not represent the opinions/standings/thoughts of **Amazon Kindle Direct** publication. No responsibility or liability is assumed by the publisher for any injury, damage or financial loss sustained to a person or property by the use of any information in this book, personal or otherwise, directly or indirectly. While every effort has been made to ensure reliability and accuracy of the information within , all liability , negligence or otherwise, by any use , misuse or abuse of the operation of any method, strategy , instruction or idea contained in the material herein is the sole responsibility of the reader. Any copyright not held by the publisher are owned by their respective authors. All information in this book is generalized and presented only for the informational purpose "as it is" without warranty or guarantee of any kind.

All trademarks and brands referred to in this book are only for illustrative purpose are the property of their respective owners and not affiliated with this publication in any way. The trademarks being used without permission don't authorize their association or sponsorship with this book.

ISBN: 9798453115426

Price:

Publishing Year 2021

Published and Printed by:

Independently Published through Amazon Kindle Direct Publication
Office Address: Amazon (India) Brigade Gateway, 8Th Floor, 26/1, Dr.Rajkumar Road, Malleshwaram (W), Bangalore- 560055
Phones: +918033273000
E-mail: amznindpr@amazon.com
Website: www.Amazon.in

Printed in India

& Various International Amazon Marketplace (Website) Through Print on Demand Technology.

A Practical Skill Development Guide

THE SKILL ARCHITECT

-75 LIFE SKILLS FOR EVERYONE – VOLUME 1

PRASAD PRAKASH TUPACHE.

B.E.(METALLURGY) , EPGDBM ,
INTERNATIONAL WELDING TECHNOLOGIST ,
SIX SIGMA GREEN BELT , ASNT LEVEL II IN
RT,UT,PT,VT,MT, EX.QUALITY HEAD .

> **INDEPENDENTLY PUBLISHED THROUGH AMAZON KINDLE DIRECT**

WITH BEST COMPLIMENTS FROM :

M/S TUPACHE CONSULTANTS

PROPRIETOR: MR.PRASAD PRAKASH TUPACHE,

GSTIN: 27AFEPT0247H1ZF, URN: UDYAM-MH260099149, SURVEY NO 79/20, SHIVRATNA COLONY, PACHPIR CHAUK, KOKANE NAGAR, KALEWADI, PIMPRI, PUNE -411017 CONTACT: 9970173983

AUTHOR:

MR. PRASAD PRAKASH TUPACHE,

B.E.(METALLURGY) ,EPGDBM , INTERNATIONAL WELDING TECHNOLOGIST , SIXSIGMA GREEN BELT .ASNT LEVEL II IN RT,UT,PT,VT,MT,EX.QUALITY HEAD .

ADDRESS:

SURVEY NO 79/20, SHIVRATNA COLONY, PACHPIR CHAUK, KOKANE NAGAR, KALEWADI, PIMPRI, PUNE 411017.

FONT SETTING: MR. PRASAD PRAKASH TUPACHE.

COVER DESIGN:

MR. PRASAD PRAKASH TUPACHE.

A) FRONT PHOTO CREDIT: CANVA.COM

B) REAR PHOTO CREDIT: CANVA.COM

PHOTO CREDIT: PROVIDENCE DOUCET, UNSPLASH.COM

THIS BOOK IS VERY VERY SINCERELY

DEDICATED TOMY DEAR,

- PARENTS
- TEACHERS
- FRIENDS
- ALL FAMILY MEMBERS
- COLLEAGUES
- PROFESSIONALS
- WORKMEN & OPERATORS
- EVERY READER

AND LAST BUT NOT LEAST

- TO MY LOVELY KIDS!

THANKS A LOT FOR YOUR CONSTANT BELEIEF!

PHOTO CREDIT: MAHESH, UNSPLASH.COM

Dear Friends,

Good Morning & Seasons Greeting!

It gives me immense pleasure to present my second English book – **The Skill Architect – 75 Life Skills For Every One, Volume 1** with all of you! This moment is special!

Consistency gives you confidence to reach great heights! While completing my first book, I was thinking about the next subject when the thought of The Skill Architect come to my mind! Why not to provide the important details of major personal & professional skills which are the backbone of all level success!

With this intention, I started writing and with Bappa's blessing, I could make it through! In This book, we are providing, sharing of useful experiences, competitive skills and general importance of adaptability to different cultures!
We hope you love & enjoy this book! Happy Reading!

PHOTO CREDIT: AMELIE NIKLAS, UNSPLASH.COM

Dear Friends,

"The Skill Architect -75 Life Skills For Every One, Volume 1" has apt illustrations in the form of number of pictures and images.

The main resource of these images is internet.

The images are downloaded for free with photo credit mentioned to its creator in respective photo as it found appropriate.

We herewith sincerely thanks all respected contributors onunsplash.com for their true support and creativity.

These images made me clarify the subject in easiest way!Thanks Again!

Yours Sincerely,

Prasad Prakash Tupache.

♦ INSPIRATIONAL ♦

IMAGE CREDIT: JANNES GLAS, UNSPLASH.COM

LETS KEEP THE GAME ON!

◆INSPIRATIONAL◆

IMAGE CREDIT: JENNY HILL, UNSPLASH.COM

SKILL INDEX

SR.NO	SKILL NAME	PAGE NO
1	ENGLISH COMMUNICATION	1-4
2	CO-ORDINATION	5-8
3	PROBLEM SOLVING	9-12
4	CONSULTING	13-16
5	GROUP DISCUSSION	17-20
6	ATTENTION TO DETAILS	21-24
7	RISK TAKING	25-28
8	DECISION MAKING	29-32
9	PERSONALITY DEVELOPMENT	33-36
10	MOTIVATION & INSPIRATION	37-40
11	VISION & MISSION SETTING	41-44
12	CHANGE MANAGEMENT	45-48
13	TRAVELLING	49-52
14	IT	53-56
15	MOBILE TECHNOLOGY	57-60
16	NEWS PAPER READING	61-64
17	TEAM BUILDING	65-68
18	DATA GENERATION	69-72
19	TECHNICAL TRAINING	73-76
20	LEADERSHIP	77-80
21	CREATIVE	81-84
22	DISCUSSION & MEETING	85-88
23	PRESENTATION	89-92
24	DEVILS ADVOCATE	93-96
25	AUDITING	97-100
26	REPORTING	101-104
27	WORK LIFE BALANCE	105-108
28	PROFITABILITY	109-112
29	VOCABULARY BUILDING	113-116
30	SUPERVISION	117-120

SKILL INDEX

SR.NO	SKILL NAME	PAGE NO
31	MANAGERIAL	121-124
32	BRAND AMBASSADOR	125-128
33	EXPLANATION	129-132
34	DEMONSTRATION	133-136
35	LOGIC APPLICATION	137-140
36	INITIATIVE	141-144
37	RELATIONSHIP MANAGEMENT	145-148
38	DEAL CRACKING	149-152
39	SPORTS	153-156
40	MORALE BOOSTER	157-160
41	LISTENING	161-164
42	INTERVIEW FACING	165-168
43	CONTINGENCY MANAGEMENT	169-172
44	ADVERSITY & SURVIVAL	173-176
45	LOAN REPAYMENT	177-180
46	MACHINE HANDLING	181-184
47	TRUST BUILDING	185-188
48	NETWORKING	189-192
49	NO FEAR ATTITUDE DEVEOPMENT	193-196
50	UNWINDING	197-200
51	RELAXATION	201-204
52	PARTYING & PARTICIPATION	205-208
53	AGENCY INTERACTION	209-212
54	MARKET READING	213-216
55	APPRAISAL MANAGEMENT	217-220
56	INVESTMENT	221-224
57	SHARING	225-228
58	NIGHT WATCHMAN	229-232
59	FUN AT WORK	233-236
60	LEAVE IT OFF	237-240

SKILL INDEX

SR.NO	SKILL NAME	PAGE NO
61	THINK LIKE CEO	241-244
62	THINK LIKE WORKMEN	245-248
63	THINK LIKE ENGINEER	249-252
64	SPRITUAL	253-256
65	STOREY TELLING	257-260
66	PRACTICING	261-264
67	ISSUE UNDERSTANDING	265-268
68	KNOWLEDGE BUILDING	269-272
69	ACTION TAKING	273-276
70	CONSTRUCTIVE DELEGATION	277-280
71	SURPRISE ELEMENT	281-284
72	ANALYSIS	285-288
73	SALARY MANAGEMENT	289-292
74	LEARN & EARN	293-296
75	TARGET SETTING	297-300

PREFACE : IDEA OF THIS BOOK

Dear Friends,

Good Morning and welcome to the simple and easy book on skill development!

It gives me immense pleasure to write this preface after completion of writing this book! The preface is about the general introduction about the book and its content, the situations experienced while writing various chapters, the state of mind at different stages of book creation and finally the satisfaction it gave me after completing the task in 61 days with 3 different volumes of this book each comprising 75 skills!

As we all know the skills are main difference makers in today's highly competitive and expanding world. When two candidates with equal qualification and experience are thought up for the single important executive position, it is the skill that decides the right choice.

Qualification has identity of technical and academic

compatibility to role desired. Experience has recognition of staying firm in the field for several years with taste of success and challenges together. This is why we say experience is the best teacher. But apart from the qualification and experience the ease with which we master our work is always known as skill!

We like tea, but we like a particular brand very much! We like to watch cricket, but we support only few players beyond our normal excitement. We like to travel, but some places always attract us to visit often? What makes it so so special! It's the beauty of the taste of the tea, the thrill of cricket certain player exhibit in the game of cricket and the divine comfort of place where we love to visit often.

Skill has such affinity to draw your customers, visitors, critics to commonly declare you as the best performer of any typical art & science. The commerce automatically follows when you keep reinventing your skills!

Noting the importance of the skills in today's life, on 26 Th Jan, 2021, I have listed 225 Skills which are generally important and necessary. Then by creating rough plan for execution started writing of this book. Every stage of this book is wonderful re- learning for me. When the format and plot of the content become familiar, the speed is picked up and by daily completion of 6-7 chapter, we could complete this made to suggest suitable illustrations and here internet image resource done the fantastic task. The idea is to have access to such numerous illustrations is simply awesome and it has shown great support to an author's creativity and experimentation.

Typical challenging phases did come while writing this book which involved too much thinking on certain topic, how to start a particular skill and how it should be kept engaging, how to put genuine real life examples which will help to understand the subject in easiest way, how to ponder thought upon a difficult skill when there are considerable technicalities involved, all these challenges are overcome with all possible determination, patience and belief on self and almighty. This makes me able to complete the book in reasonable good time as per my own understanding.

Being the second book, the experience of writing was comparatively easy and I have witnessed improved confidence after writing every 100 pages in about weeks' time! The satisfaction of going through this numerical journey was awesome and achieving 900 pages was a big personal satisfaction while on the go. We have tried our best to present the most practical experiences to make this book user friendly. The narration used here is simple, easy and readable. We have taken care to highlight special paragraph from the skill chapters to emphasize certain aspects of the chapter easily!

Friends, every creation has its own accomplishment and its own limits. Human element always plays the role of constant improvement and thoughtful revision of what can be done more to make it more easy and simple. We are aware that there may be certain shortfalls, some errors or some different opinions 180 degree opposite! But friends, please let us share with you that individuality, freedom and experimentation has always convinced me to go ahead and put the skill details in front of you to have easy and simple understanding.

In case of any concern or if some thoughts found to be too bold, we can always discuss for more clarification. We have tried our best to think in depth before putting it for you!

Hope you all like this book!

We wish you happy reading!

Yours Friendly

– Prasad Prakash Tupache.

LETS START

SKILL 1 : ENGLISH COMMUNICATION SKILL

PHOTO CREDIT :KRAKEN IMAGES, UNSPLASH.COM

Namaste Dear Friends!!!

Warm welcome & Heartiest Congratulations to meet here!

This feeling is simply amazing!

We assure best interaction & connection with this book!

With the introduction of colonial culture to build Business Empire, language has played a crucial role. Since the native language of British's was English, same is spread all across the peculiar colonial culture to facilitate business dealings! The development , acceptance and usage of English as business language is happened in structured way through education , cultural inclusion and executive level practical's to spread across the generations since last 200 years . This is history and history has taught us that English is widely used business language!

> *"We are in 21 st century now and civic development with English language is widespread with inclusion of English in school syllabus from standard 1! The generations growing in next 10 years will be having excellent command over this language since their association is much deeper and stronger. "*

But what about the generation which is not very conversant about this necessary skill? They may know how to write in English, How to express in English, How to read in English but may not know How to talk in negotiations, How to talk in appraisals and How to talk in networking events! You can't talk in same fashion and tone at these different events which happen regularly in normal lifetime. This book will provide some of the tips to polish your English speaking & communication skill easily & systematically. English communication in business is equal to clear, quiet and neat dialogue with active listening and sharp responding to have a candid interaction.

Following is the proven practical way to improve our English Communication Skill:

- Practice Salutations in most polite way.
- Use right greetings.
- First listen carefully, and then initiate the dialogue from your side.
- Brake the ice whenever meets with new person.
- Business chat can start with main points of discussion which later grows into detailed know-how of topic of discussion.
- At the end of the discussion generally a positive agreement happens with interacting parties.
- In case of disagreements, never close the deal from your side, keep it open. Business has lots of uncertainties!
- Always stay positive during dialogue. If not confident about some specific details, ask for some time to revert and respond.
- New connection goes well with formal discussion. After one or two meetings, people generally prefer to have informal dialogue adhering to basic business communication skills.
- Business communication is all about status update, commitment towards timely completion of projects, suggestions of options in case of adversities and referencing for necessary delegation and supervision.

- Business vocabulary is about practical English speaking and it seldom uses classical English, so stay simple, clear and expressive in talks!
- Practice the language via group chat, newspaper reading and listening, practicing alone and practicing with friends.
- Errors in speaking in initial stage are very very common. Record your speech and observe the delivery of dialogues.
- Think in English, draw some figures and set the connection of discussion topic to decide right sequence of communication.
- Apart from basic grammar take care of punctuations, expressions and pauses. Pause works well to have impactful communication.
- General challenge is with use of tense. Read novels and watch movies with subtitles to clear doubts.
- Language is emotional connection. Make sure, you know the meaning of words before their usage. They make huge impact.
- Speak softly, it goes long way.
- Respect other person's English skill; he may not be as fluent as you are. Understand each other to have positive interaction with bullet points.
- Practice! Practice! Practice!
- Never give up! It take some time to learn this skill, it come with experience, keep talking, start writing and listen attentively. We hope, this information is exciting! Let's pause here! ✍

SKILL 2 : CO-ORDINATION SKILL

PHOTO CREDIT : MAX WINKLER, UNSPLASH.COM

Dear Friends,

" Business co-ordination is a simple game of collection & distribution with you standing in the middle ! You may be collecting objects, money or data ! The task is to distribute it to right channel , right person and at right time!"

Business is people paradise and there is different kind of people generally seen. People are sincere, innovative, creative , expressive, introvert, supportive, aggressive, demanding , funny , humorous, strategic ,generous, clever , shy , arrogant , defensive , positive ,strong , quiet and so many other attributes are found when we deal with people in a typical business environment at different time!

> "When it comes to co-ordination skill , we have to consider the first very very important aspect to have this skill is the ability to understand and apply the particular hierarchy in the organization. "

In normal scenario, you have to deliver your duty by completing assigned tasks & responsibility. Tasks are nothing but small work steps which ensure realization of particular status of the product or service. Let's take a small material transaction example: You have to order a 100 meter pipe from internal stores to shop floor. Here how it will be co-ordinated by a shop supervisor:

- Check the stock in material availability record and in case of shortage, initiate the indent to stores. Stores will check their stock, if not available, will communicate to buyer and supervisor.

- Generally buyer maintains safe stock level but in case of shortages, they have to plan through urgent

indenting With proper approvals.
- With availability of pipe, store keeper will issue the material to shop supervisor which will be checked by receipt and shop QC at their respective workstations.
- Receipt QC & Shop QC will ensure, supplier material is correct and in case of any dispute they will raise alarm in system to ensure its return to store, call to supplier and getting right material for production.
- With this checkpoint, supervisor will accept the 100 meter pipe from store, will store in his inventory and keep record of its consumption through shop QC.
- After this recording material is physically handed over to workmen for its usage as per drawing dimension & location.
- Workmen will measure & fit the material at right location and join it with appropriate process practiced. He will return remaining pipe to material issuer in shop.
- Shop QC will keep record of this remaining pipe for any future use of that much small length with transfer & stamping of its identification no.
- This closes activity of co-ordination done by shop supervisor with store keeper, store manager, buyer, Quality and workmen along with his supervising production manager.

Few tips for successful co-ordination:

1) Know your role.
2) Know the organization structure and reporting authorities of individual and group, teams.
3) Communicate both verbally and in writing with appropriate action details.
4) Allow time required for the transaction.
5) Follow up for status and any other input
6) On availability, delegate the task to downstream team member, get work done.
7) In case of deviations, discontinuity or problems talk to immediate executive, if not resolved, move together to decisionmaking authority.
8) Plan your schedule according to priorities.
9) Plan for shift, day, week, and month in advance and understand the availability status with other team members.
10) Make sure you get timely update of status with constant formal & informal communication.

Co-ordination skill is one of the vital business skill and at any point of our career, we have to acquire this skill with comfort and ease as we progresses career ladder!

Let's take a pause here! ✍

SKILL 3 : PROBLEM SOLVING SKILL

PHOTO CREDIT : NEONBRAND, UNSPLASH.COM

Dear Friends!!!

Warm welcome to the problem solving skill chapter!

> " A well-defined problem leads to its best solution ! Problem structure comprises major pain points and minor miss outs which makes problem look bigger & larger "

Friends, when we are doing business, we are earning money by resolving people problems. We are providing intellectual solutions to people general pain points to make their daily life easy with the use of scientifically developed methods and customized services created by noting individual customer's requirement.

Human race is unique and they are constantly developing there selves to explore all possibilities that science & technology offers in nature. While doing this, we are meeting with some fantastic innovations of mankind while we are also observing some unexpected challenges like environmental degradation because of incorrect application & spread of some of the technological innovations.

In such grossly turbulent time , it become necessary to have basic problem solving skills to overcome the fear of unexpected failure , delays in normal work and to have peace of mind that comes with a systematic resolution of problem .

Let it be normal daily life or a typical month end situation, we face some problems irrespective of our age. Status or education. The more we may differ about problem solving concept is our ability to look at it!

Problems can be technical, behavioral, time bound or open ended, simple or complex, can be tackled individually, independently or with the help and support from a team, problems are meant to resolve!

Let's work out a practical problem solving approach for everybody!

Practical Problem Solving Approach:

- ✓ Define the problem statement.
- ✓ Definition must involve major pain point, quantum of loss or delay and its dire need of resolution.
- ✓ Brake the problem statement into stepwise resolution of 5M's of management.
- ✓ If the problem is related with **people**, discuss with concern team to know their limitation and suggest best alternative that will satisfy their work conditions or concern and at the same time the solution is technically correct & feasible.
- ✓ If the problem is related to **machine**, look for repair, time bound monitoring and analyze the performance and performance gap. Add simulators that enhance the performance, block the irregularity in the system by appropriate cleaning, refitting and testing at no load condition.
- ✓ If the problem is related with **method**, take a call with all participants and suggest new way of working with addition of required remedy. Communicate clearly, get people trained with new method and observe the difference in performance.

  If the problem is related with **measurement**, adopt a more enhanced instrument, check people skill of handling the equipment, check status of instrument for its calibration.

- ✓ If the problem is related to **material** of construction, study the material in detail for its microstructure, physical and chemical properties, heat treatments and performance under normal service environment. If required, use alternative material with the help of list of standard material specifications.
- ✓ If the problem is related with **money**, money can be arranged with loan, various government and private financial schemes and can be borrowed if amount is okay for its payee based on mutual trust and professional relation.

Positive approach in life does wonders in solving various problems. Constant reading & update of business event help us to take right decision. These right decisions make our work easy. This easiness avoids major problems.

Problems can be resolved by avoiding it, discussing & acting on it, collaborating with concern team members and in last stage by approaching designated authorities which can be legal or statutory. But for every problem there is solution!

We can develop problem solving skill by directly counting with problems at ground zero. It's the best way to know problem genuinely. It boosts confidence & knowledge! Let's take a pause here. ✍

SKILL 4 : CONSULTING SKILL

PHOTO CREDIT : ROLAND SAMUEL, UNSPLASH.COM

Dear Friends,

Warm welcome to meet again on this page! This feeling is simply amazing!

We assure best interaction & connection with this book!

> " A shivering trainee engineer approached Mr. Seth . He told about extreme cold out there in the field and because of which he was fearing to have cracks in the weld , actually he had seen one ,during trial run on the test piece . Mr. Seth talked with trainee and suggested him to refer the respective WPS of joining material to note Preheat temperature, interpass temperature and post weld heat treatment which will result into crack free seamless high quality welding irrespective of cold and environmental challenges! Trainee went happily as he got the solution for his fear ! "

Although Mr. Seth is an indicative name and trainee engineer is just any newcomer in any field, there are such knowledgeable people in every field who with their wide experience, practical knowledge and descent application resolve complex issues swiftly and regularly. This much sought after skill is known as consulting skill.

Whenever there is need of technical prudence and expertise, consultant will have red carpet treatment from their clients and solution seekers. They will visit the problem site with formal request, will analyze the status, will observe the process, will study its variable, and will judge the relation between system under observation and its impacting surrounding. Based on this study and using their field experience and expertise , in some special cases by using their networking skill with other field expert , they will suggest the remedy , get it implemented and hand over the project with accurate and timely resolution with right professional fees . This is what practical consultancy majorly.

But can we become consultant on joining? Typically No but in Films Yes! Ha, Ha! Let's understand stepwise journey to imbibe the skillset of consulting.

The Classic Consultant Approach:

- ➢ When you start as a newcomer, observe the technical relation of various machines. This can be done by noting the performance indicators at different practical settings of the machine.
- ➢ A static machine will give you complete knowledge about its component, their fitment, their dimensions, their function and theirorientation.
- ➢ When the same machine is in action, with proper safety precautions like wearing face shield, hand gloves and aprons, machine can be seen in action mode. This observation will provide knowledge about inherent mechanism.
- ➢ The next step is to imagine and apply the conditions with peculiar parts presence, absence or malfunction. E.g. if indicator light is not lit when reaching certain speed or temperature, what will happen? If quantity of oil in oil tank is dropped below minimum, how machine will stop?

If there is short circuit with electric assembly, how mechanical system can be isolated and protected?
- Such critical thinking will give you experience of noting live problems in working machines.
- With sufficient presence in the field, you will understand these problems can be resolved with repair, replacement or rework by using suggested tools and tackles.
- Once this technique is understood, you have to try your own hands on such machines to know about which screw need to tight lightly and how to adjust spanner in intricate locations!
- These hands on experience will add to your kitty wide pool of knowledge of tackling difficult situations.
- Practice this skill till you achieve expertise.
- Resolution of problems will create your identity as problem solver and people from different field may approach you.
- Your technical & tactful decision to these people will become your consulting skill and you will become a genuine consultant!
- With kind of problems, you have to improve on this skill and with growing years you will become a one stop solution for business consulting!

Let's take a pause here! ✍

SKILL 5 : GROUP DISCUSSION SKILL

PHOTO CREDIT : MARGARIDA CSILVA, UNSPLASH.COM

Hello Friends!!!

We meet each other many times, on many occasions, for different reasons and for different interactions. As we all know, this kind of meeting is better known as informal chat or friendly affairs of memories and pranks which is loved by everybody! But what is a group discussion means? Let's jump straight on this subject!

Friends, in life we encounter with some of the situations in which the way we express ourselves decides the result of our interaction. A shy, soft spoken person may be taken for ride by a smart, selfish and clever counterpart in some of the daily life dealings. So, one need to be clear, firm and logical in their interaction with people when they are discussing personal or professional matters.

> " Group discussion is an art and science of expression of ideas, opinions and questions in front of team of participating and non-participating team members! It is the most professional way of putting your judgment on subject under discussion.
>
> Always remember a logical and respectful participant wins the discussion and hearts ! So be descent, thoughtful and genuinely humorous in any group discussion . Humor resolves argumentsduring group discussion !"

Generally, subjects chosen for group discussion are open ended matters in which candidates or participants inclination, interest and conscience is judged with respect to other participant. It's not necessary to win every argument, it's not necessary to have several punches and catchy slogans, nor it required to be aggressive and over enthusiastic!

All it matters is situational delivery of opinions when somebody is putting the best thought on the table. It requires patient listening of other participant when they are expressing and involve in the discussion with your unique know-how of the matter. A silence in case of unknown situation is always welcome rather than putting wrong theories and postulates. The thoughts need to be precise, pure and practical. At times, one can involve in argument but release has to be respectful and noteworthy.

Let's check a simple checklist before entering into group discussion!

Group Discussion Checklist:

- ✓ Be presentable, warm and attentive.
- ✓ Understand the subject of group discussion clearly.
- ✓ Derive your own judgment of subject and presume your stand on whether you are supporting the subject or opposing the subject or you prefer to stay neutral or in rare case you not want to take part into group discussion as it's not in your general ethics and principles.
- ✓ Your every stand will be correct till you have its tactful, real, logical justification or answer.
- ✓ Avoid vague expressions, be real.
- ✓ Input humor in between.
- ✓ Agree to best thought and praise openly.
- ✓ Support a participant in case you know what he want to say, but somehow not able to express in

specific words, if you guessed it, fill that gap of incomplete expressions. This will create your presence as a considerate team member. You may involve in the discussion with expression, "May be my friend want to say..." and then receive his nod! This completes the communication and present the discussion thought in meaningful way.

- ✓ In the event of serious disagreements, agree to disagree. Group discussions are like parliamentary affairs, everybody has freedom of expression and everybody has right of not getting bullied by some extreme opinions during discussion. The decorum is important and we need to maintain the clean dais.
- ✓ It's not winning or loss which is important, it's the presence, compassion, support and tactful reluctance which get noted by team.
- ✓ One common gesture, love people, love individual thinking patterns and is a strong collaborator. Try to conclude the discussion on fair note and mutual understanding with professional handshakes!
- ✓ Last but not least, forget the discussion when it ends. We have to always think on new topics!

Friends, hope you find out this topic interesting. Always keep exchanging thoughts, view and tactful details with accurate figures to make your point noteworthy.

Let's take a pause here! ✍

SKILL 6 : ATTENTION TO DETAILS SKILL

PHOTO CREDIT : MARCUS WINKLER, UNSPLASH.COM

Good Morning Friends!

Welcome to this new chapter, attention to details skill!

Let's have a math's treat:

1) 5+2=8
2) 14-11=4
3) 7x 8=57
4) 15/5=2

Yes, you are correct, the answers are wrong! They should be as follow:

1) 5+2=7
2) 14-11=3
3) 7x 8=56
4) 15/5=3

But why this example here?

Friends, welcome to the chapter of attention to details skill. One of the most sought after skill in any industry especially technically aligned fields such as design, research & development, quality, production. The team working in this field is fed up with various kinds of data in their working life. Which can be a drawing, a commercial document, a standard or specification, in all such events they need to go into details to understand the requirements of the project, mandatory points of the project to maintain the strict compliance? Any miss out, lacuna or error has great cost measure associated with it as a part of contract and as per general business understanding, so when it's your turn, you need to have keen eye for all details of that particular activity.

In above example, we have seen a typical math equation, where we have taught in the school, and the basics of calculus. These answers are stored in our memory and when we see any deviation to standard universal mathematical answer, we say it is wrong. Now in normal life, such reference can be anything, we have to study the reference material in details with all its pros & cons and then we have to compare the sample or samples under consideration to arrive at right decision. More is the accuracy of judgment and prediction, more successful we will be!

> *"Attention to details means knowing the essential and non-essential aspects of any subject. Essential aspect has priority of selection over non-essential aspects before making a firm decision. An error in non-essential aspect may not have serious impact on overall result but error in essential aspect create major worries in decision making. Keen & detailed thought process on all aspect generate a sound inclination towards a fact based & tactful decision making skill."*

How this skill is mastered? Let's take a look:

Steps to master attention to details skill:

1. Receive 100% information necessary for decision making.
2. Study all documents, figures and tables for their indicative figures; inter relation and importance in decision making.
3. Look for shape, size and technical dimensional details. Chances of miss out lies in this section.
4. Quantity & price can be checked by tally method. If

there is error in quantity, tally will not match.

5. Comparison of standard reference material with available sample is main, when seen clearly, we can find out the differences easily.
6. When we understand reference material and as we do practice with more samples, we memories the sample thoroughly and hence we can take faster, accurate and easy decisions.
7. In case of financial dealing, more attention need to be given on exchange rates, location of decimal points and no of zeros in typical high value transaction and " In words" amount. A total tally of all these details leads to a successful decision on monetary affair.
8. In case of drawing study, we need to understand projection views of the object, meaning of every section line and its viewing direction, pictorial symbols and notes, tolerance table, code of construction, design details, bill of material and parts catalogue. These checks will lead to correct decision on part building.
9. Record major details as notes which will become handy when it is required to refer frequently.
10. Discuss the details with concern team members; hence in case you miss something, they may help you to arrive at right decision as a team.

We hope you find this approach helpful. Practice makes man perfect. Hence practice to great extent to have ease of dealing with attention to details!

SKILL 7 : RISK TAKING SKILL

PHOTO CREDIT : CLARK YOUNG, UNSPLASH.COM

Good Morning Friends,

Hope you are doing great!

It was last over of final match & 12 runs were needed from 6 balls. First two balls went without a single, now pressure was mounted on, the on strike batsman as equation was changed to 12 runs in 4 balls. He was the only batsman on the field as his non-strike end partner was regular bowler with normal batting skills. On next ball he managed to take double. Now equation changed to 3 balls, 10 runs. For next ball, he took the risk to come forward and hit out of the ground. He succeeded and got a fantastic sixer. Now equation 2 balls 4 runs. Next ball was a deadly Yorker, which he survived. Now last ball with requirement of 4 to win and 3 to tie, double to loose. He seen the field spacing, he talked with partner, he also seen towards dressing room. The bowler was consistently able to swing the bowl and question in his mind was whether he will put a Yorker or an out swinger or an in swinger or a slower one. He made his relevant plan for each delivery and took his strike. Surpassing his expectation, the bowler bowled a mid-height bouncer which he pulled down the fence to record a stunning victory! Had he not took the risk of coming forward and hit a sixer, the result of match could be totally different!

"Friends , risk is nothing but a thoughtful call taken under consideration for a brave result or outcome in response to a tricky and challenging situation ! There is great uncertainty and nothing can be predicted in advance. All it matters is our ability to believe in our strengths, our ability to cope up with our weaknesses , understand the strength & weakness of counterpart and decide a strategy to overcome the situational challenge with the bold steps in the form of calculated risk ensuring great success in case of right call and least loss in case of unfortunate failure !"

Business risk involve care of finances, care of people , care of costlier machines and their handling , environmental and political aspects which changes as per business environment . In all such cases, an entrepreneur has to develop an operating system which is process oriented, which has performance benchmarks, system of checks and balances and above all an indomitable team spirit with which they can become winner in any challenging situations.

We generally fear for loss of people or money as to earn it again, we need very very hard efforts and we are not sure, whether we will get same quality of people or same price for changed features. Also there is fear of failure that if everything is gone wrong, we will be unable to survive. This fear leads to move towards a risk free decision making and a stagnant way of leaving. We cut short our chances of all directional growth by securing ourselves under an umbrella of supposed security.

The risk takers world has many challenges and difficulties in the path. Every difficulty shows two options, either to stuck in the middle or overcome the difficulty with application of knowledge, wisdom, experience and strength. Risk taker learn every day and as time passes he become familiar with kind of pressure associated and the remedy to tackle it. In this way , his genuine interest to take risks present himself as a hardworking , long lasting individual who never afraid to take risks. Let's see typical steps in building the risk taking skill.

Risk Taking Model:

- Believe in your strength and past achievements.
- Train your mind about the prevailing situation .The prevailing situation is temporary and you will come out of it eventually with the help of quality of your efforts & decisions.
- Understand all pros in case of success of decision.
- Estimate type of losses in case of a false decision.
- Analyze the impact of false decision on other life events.
- Discuss the decision with concern team members; take them into your confidence.
- Persuade consistently and arrive at logical agreement.
- Devise plan of risk handling and mitigation.
- Take the risk and put your all energy to make your decision true a successful.
- Observe the situational dynamics and improvise according to situation to deliver aright response.
- The risk will be reduced as you achieve great control over situation and with right time you will win over the situation.
- Record the decision for future queries and stay prepared with necessary resources.
- Never fear for failure, never let success go into hands of wild thoughts. Stay humble, lively and relaxed in all situations, which is the base for sound risk taking. Let's take a pause here! ✍

SKILL 8 : DECISION MAKING SKILL

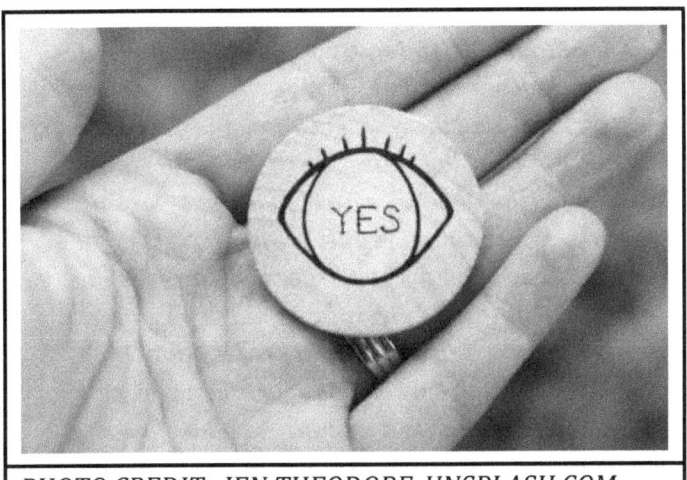

PHOTO CREDIT : JEN THEODORE, UNSPLASH.COM

Hello Friends,

Good Morning, hope you are doing fine!

Life is all about right decisions and favorite choices. The ultimate success of life is measured on the basis of peace of mind achieved out of successful, durable decisions of life. Decisions make us and also brake us. It's our intuition which guides us to take right decision. Let's go into more details in this chapter of major skill known as decision making skill.

> " Decisions are thoughtful outcome of appliedknowledge , facts and tact's.
> When this choice
> matches with reality , decisions result into a success.When this judgment and choice mis matches with reality , the decision become a failure . So to arrive at right decision what is essential is the awareness about ground reality which depicts right picture to have accurate choice. Decisions has both short termand long terms impact on one's personal and professional life , hence due care need to be taken in case of important life decisions such has favorite profession, preferred qualification, genuine interest,job location , business development , marriage , child care and their upbringing , elders care and their well-being , health status and its wellness, diet& eating habits and general leisure activities.
> Everywhere we have to take decisions based on ourchoices and preferences. "

In student life, we have to take decision about choice of course. In such decisions, we have to look upon our natural interest in that subject. A subject look boring but has good financial potential , such choice will give you money but in long term will not provide zeal to experiment , feel to explore your talent and thrill to conquer the platform with your innovative ideas.

There are typical situations in business life. You have to interact with foreign delegates on project status or facility expansion. You may have to discuss salary restructuring with your staff because of enhanced performance. You may have to procure new material which you are buying first time. In this entire respective situation, you decide to meet customer with updated details of project with handy calculations justifying the proper usage of their investments and trust engagement. You decide to give descent rise which will make your staff happy and motivated to deliver their best. You may decide to explore new market or you may take help of your friend who is regularly doing such transactions. In each case, you decide something to arrive at right conclusion before investing your resources, money and time. This skill of making right choice is known as decision making skill.

Decisions can be structured and open ended. Structured decisions has definite proven path and its outcome is predictable. Such as to refill of a typical LPG gas cylinder of 14.7 Kg at its refill station, the time required is 5 minutes with standard refilling arrangement. Now let it be 1 cylinder or 1000, the time will be same ,hence here operator has to just arrange cylinder at refill location , make sure it is connected with preset gas filling station and observe its weight till it reaches preset cylinder weight . Once reaches the desired level, he has to stop refilling and arrange other cylinder. The decision is structured. In non-structured decisions, the outcome is unpredicted and we have to constantly monitor the status about successful decision making. E.g. decision to implement vaccination drive. We have to constantly keep track of successful vaccination till we achieve desired immunity to disease under consideration.

Let's point out typical decision making skill path:

Decision Making Path:

1) Understand the situation in which you have to take right decision.

2) Maintain cool head full of practical options & choices.

3) Gather data, acquire knowledge, read similar case studies and recommendations and then make your choice.

4) Take time to arrive at right decision. Once decided stay firm and confident. Never change unless it is completely acceptable to you.

5) Confusion creates delay and chances of errors. SO stay clear and calm in challenging phases of decision implementation.

6) Some decision impact major processes. Consult right person, before taking a riskier decision.

7) Learn from good & incorrect decisions.

8) Always develop positive inclination towards calculated risk taking, careful handling and descent execution of business activities.

Hope you find this input helpful. Let's take a pause here!

SKILL 9 : PERSONALITY DEVELOPMENT SKILL

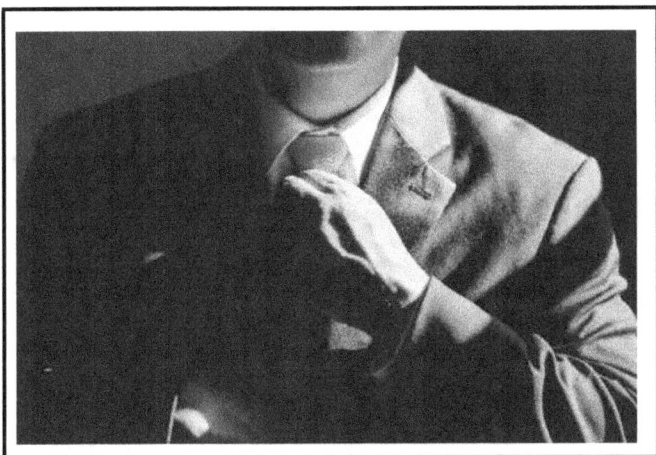

PHOTO CREDIT :BEN ROSETT , UNSPLASH.COM

Dear Friends!!!

Good Morning & welcome to this chapter of personality development!

We all love movies, it may be English, Hindi or any regional language movie. When we like movie, may be because of its script, direction or acting, we watch it again & again. Sometimes we imitate famous actors and sometimes we also get inspired to some different stuff by recreating our creative potential.

But what attracts us from movie? The first and foremost answer is the flimsy characters and their larger than life presence on the screen. We all know that stories are imaginary and characters are artificial, yet we believe in story and sequence shown in scenes and get engaged ourselves for 2-3 hours just to get entertain. The experience is funful and exciting, that's what a movie make a successful presentation.

> *" Personality is peculiar feature of individual . It's the unique presentation of attire, speech and expression . Everybody has a special personality which defines their identity ."*

Business and personality has close relation. Many a time you have to talk in front of large no of people, many a time you have to deliver inaugural , motivating , debatable speeches according to business situations , many a time you have to liaison with high profile customers, officials and external agencies. In all such instances the way you present yourself defines your personality. A positive approach, neat & clean attire, descent professional talk, accurate application of mindful expression, ability to agree to different thought and putting our thought in between discussion create influence of your personality. This influence flows into business network to create your social image and identity. Once this image is accepted by large masses, your brand name is sufficient to create an impression of your offering, which may be a product, service or your own branding.

There are typical personal attributes. Firm handshake , active listening , correct mannerism , ability to give & take respect, warmth and joyfulness , broad thinking about life events, deep understanding of business decisions and interpersonal relation management , all these points leads to develop a widely acceptable renowned person .

Not to forget, the way we eat, the way we travel, the way we compete also attributes to our personality. In today's world, you have to be a tech savvy person. Your skill to use various gazettes effortlessly creates a long lasting impression.

Let's check some must have of a good, charming personality.

Attributes of a Good Charming Personality:

- They are open person with wide vision.
- They respect and adhere time.
- They value every relation, every individual, and every association.
- They speak clear, clean and genuine.
- They treat everyone with respect, love and care, they are affectionate to others.
- They are responsible and accept the mistakes

graciously and improve to avoid repetition .
- They wait till their turn comes, when it's their turn, they perform to best of their capability.
- They are equal opportunity players and they support positive workforce competition.
- They foster an impeccable team spirit whatever may be their role in the organization .They get attached with their role and atmosphere thoroughly.
- They refuse self-talk and allow others to express their view freely and constructively.
- They support in crisis and allow freedom to take risks in business decisions.
- They have a large heart with ability to pardon mistakes made out of normal work pressures.
- They know human resource has feelings and they make it sure, everybody feel part of the organization in which they are serving. They are accommodative.
- On lighter side, they are happy, humorous and have fluent oratory skills which create an immediate connection with their followers.
- They remember everyone with their first name and insist to call them by first name.
- They love challenges and they live a life full of pride, satisfaction and glory in their chosen field.
- They are social contributors and help to large extent.
- They read a lot! We hope, you enjoyed this topic.

Let's take a pause here!

SKILL 10 : MOTIVATION & INSPIRATION SKILL

PHOTO CREDIT :THIS IS ENGINEERING, UNSPLASH.COM

Hello Friends ,

Nice to see you here !

It was a fully packed auditorium with distinguished dignitaries on the dais. Kamal has to deliver a motivational speech on Employment & Entrepreneurship . Everybody was so excited to hear his speech because Kamal has recently won the Global Public Speaker award which is hugely popular and inspirational for young aspiring minds . Kamal started the speech and crowd mesmerized with his examples, quotes and gestures. There were claps , laughs and continuous roar of his name . The speech was simply amazing and really motivational .

Let's see the journey & struggle behind this success. Before delivering motivational speech , Kamal was a banker and was doing a comfortable 9 to 5 job . He was avid reader and creative writer. He often likes to talk with some funny expressions when he was with his friends. At times he used to consult in a very very special way. Because of his generous advice and clear opinion, his friends fondly respect him so much that they used to take his advice in every important situation of their life. He was so much reliable and genuine.

Noting his quality of selfless expression, in one of the cultural gathering in the town, one of his friends requested him to talk a bit in front of local audience to deliver a speech on latest technology and education. Preparation was Kamal's main focus point. Kamal prepared for the speech for 2 day and delivered a fantastic speech at the event. Everybody was so happy that he resolved lots of doubts and queries effortlessly. In fact many young minds inspired by his speech and decided to look seriously on their future career prospects with the help of input shared by Kamal.

Since then, he started performing at various events held at local, district, state and national level and this award was the result of his three years of dedication to this wonderful inherent skill. With steady source of income and all round popularity, Kamal quit his job to become full time motivational speaker. He has written 5 books on importance of motivation and inspiration in life, career challenges and role of our thinking, advanced people skill, society and public speaking and discovery of confidence. Three of his books are e-commerce bestsellers attracting young minds. Oh, what an achievement this is!

Friends, this story is imaginary but this is also true to the extent that it is relevant to some of the famous motivational speaker's success story.

> *"Inspiration is ability to drive yourself through any situation while motivation is ability to inspire someone else with your effective expressions which are full of logic, concern and easy acceptance."*

People have feelings, moods and mental barriers. They have some doubts, fears and clarity concerns. Very often they are stubborn in their thinking style and reluctant to try out other side of the challenge. The skill to motivate imbibes a sense of trust with such people. It allows such thinkers to understand importance of rationale thinking. It resolves their doubts by introducing to their own strength points. This skill makes them move to next best level of their performance. The skill of inspiration often guides us to try new avenues. This skill creates better version of yourself. Ability to inspire is basic leadership trait and its fully practical acceptability. Let's look at some points of motivation & inspiration:

Some Inspirational & Motivational Stuff:

- Sportsman, Musicians, Singers, and Actors goes through very very hard grind before they become successful and well known. It's their ability to get inspired and motivated which keeps them moving in uncertain environment.
- Renowned scientist, philanthropic surgeons and successful industrialist went through hard labour of mind & body before they create their larger than life image.
- Every special child undergoes strict struggle to lead a normal life before he become an achiever in life.
- Not only human but animals do struggle hard for their life. Its natural instinct which make them going.
- Struggle keeps us alive .Inspiration touches our soul while motivation give us return gift of enhanced confidence. So always stay positive and inspired.

We hope, you have enjoyed this topic. Inspiration and motivation is must have ability of a successful person. Practice this skill with sheer determination and genuine contribution.

Let's take a pause here! ✍

SKILL 11: VISION & MISSION SETTING SKILL

PHOTO CREDIT : DANIEL GUERRA, UNSPLASH.COM

Good Noon Dear Friends,

Welcome to this new chapter of vision & mission setting skill.

Long back in year 1999, after my SSC result, I decided to pursue Engineering. Actually the dream to become an engineer was seen in fifth standard at the age of 10 and accordingly I have enrolled for intermediate technical education course taught on one day of the week from standard 8th. What was the fascination about this profession ? Its shear magic of science , technological advances and thrill to explore something new constantly . It took 2006 to get formal first class degree & a decent job , it took 2018 to become Head of the Quality department while 2021 to become independent technical & creative authorpreneur. The journey till now is part of my own little vision of becoming a successful engineer with mission of constant learning . I am happy with my progress and continuing my best efforts to explore new challenges and new possibilities. This example is shared just to simplify the concept of vision & mission setting! Personal recognition or

> " Friends , everybody aspire to become a better & successful person in their life journey . The path of success is different for different individual . Some aspirant get instant success while some requires enormous efforts to win the honor of accomplishment . Dreams are fulfilled with utmost determination, clear fundamentals and well defined course of effective actions . Vision helps you to foresee the desired long term destination while mission get you there with systematic approach and effective performance steps. Its human endeavor to deal with difficulties and obstacles with "Can do " approach which defines their individual connection with final vision and mission statement !"

flattery was never on mind!

How to set vision statement :

1) Determine what you want to be or how your contribution to society should be useful.
2) These two factors will form the base of your vision statement.
3) Remember vision statement has to be large purpose, wide spread application and ability to stay in the game amidst challenging times.
4) Vision statement in this way is like radar which always guides you toward right direction of your journey.
5) Make vision statements inclusive so people can associate themselves easily while doing their job.
6) The larger perspective of vision statement has to be linked with individual and group performance in decently articulated words which are inspirational, clear and well known to masses.
7) Vision statement is like a guide and hence it's simple but meaningful.
8) At any point of journey, vision statement need to create feeling of achievement, sense of satisfaction and zeal to contribute to a higher level.
9) Usage of less used words to be avoided and focuses to be given to include simple meaningful words that can be understood by layman to consultant quickly, clearly and easily.
10) Inclusiveness and cultural bonding is another purpose of setting vision statement. Vision

statement indirectly reflects the organizational culture , hence it needs to be mirror of what is practiced in normal work environment.

How to set mission statement :

1) Align your mission statement to the core of your vision statement.
2) Define a clear & systematic path to achieve your final goal.
3) Develop process , people and market in accordance to time bound expansion of business in both long term and short run.
4) Set up your systems which can be technical , financial or people systems to ensure effective operational dynamics and humane interaction.
5) Allocate best time management skill in mission statement itself ,which will make every stakeholder responsible for their time with the organization in a best possible way.
6) Clarity is second noun of mission statement . Make sure mission statement defines the essential performance indicators.
7) Don't set ideal expectations, include practical expectations which people will love to exceed often.

Friends , mission and vision setting skill is a vital skill . Imagine your best version all-time!

Let me take a pause here!

SKILL 12 : CHANGE MANAGEMENT SKILL

PHOTO CREDIT : USGS, UNSPLASH.COM

Dear Friends ,

Grand welcome to one of the most important skill chapter – The change management skill .

    State of the matter is a physical concept by which we classify universal material as solid , liquid and gaseous . With application of temperature these state of matters are altered to get desired state of the matter which is useful for general day-to- day applications.

We need electricity , we converted static energy stored in water to create electricity , and we changed water

> " Change management is systematic approach to note the change with respect to existing practice . Change management deals with communication , action and endorsement of change with respective stakeholders. In change management , supervising authorities guide individual or group to facilitate with the change , to respond with doubts and queries and emerge as change agent .
>
> By devoting some time which can be in days, week or month or in special terms years , the change become conversant and can be called as normal practice !Most of the time change brings good result in personal & professional life! So always be ready and flexible for every change ! "

and world also . When we were in need of fast vehicle , we searched concept of wheel , steam engine and subsequently excelled up to bullet train exceeding speed barriers of past . With advent of communication technology we changed the way we speak with each other. Starting from telegram, gramophone to latest slick gazette , we changed a lot . Generations of people evolved with constant changes in their development . So, we can state , every human being is capable of being a change agent by which he can contribute to society in great extent . Let's spread some light on challenges of change management .

How Sankalp managed a job switch change :

Sankalp is a mechanical engineer with 5 years of work experience in a manufacturing organization . He is excellent in drafting and design of automobiles and currently he has received a new offer from a reputed MNC's new operation in the different city with a descent rise and promotion to new managerial role . Sankalp informed his superior about the change and requested his release from their side .

Sankalp joined new organization in new city . The new company HR Executive helped him to find the nearest accommodation in new town and also managed his food arrangement with nearby chain of reputed caterers in that area. Being a bachelor , Sankalp preferred shared accommodation with company friends and from day one he started to go office with his new friends in this organization .

In his probation period of six month , he captured the process details and demonstrated his experience to make processes simple and more productive . He participated in several design competitions organized by sector in that area and emerged as winner & runner up at two instances .

Sankalp was friendly with everybody . He took part in most of the cultural and technical event happened during that year . Thus along with new job , Sankalp build new relations .

His hometown was 100 Km farther than previous location but still he managed to visit his home 2 times in 6 months' probation on consecutive holidays and weekly offs.

After 3 months , Sankalp got familiar with locals and he started mixing with local cultural group and few social organizations. Sankalp is a regular blood donor and a trekking enthusiast . He joined the famous " KilleShahi " trekking troop and visited 3 forts in six months' time .

His appraisal went fantastic and he got his confirmation with yet another performance bonus and excellence reward. This made him happy of his achievement and now management is thinking to allocate him greater responsibilities in coming semester. Sankalp is happy about this development and putting great effort to cherish this trust !

Friends ,this is the best change management story one can expect in their job life . But remember the grass is not always green and every cloud has silver lining . So learn from success as well as challenges. Life is all about noting , managing and accepting variety of changes .

So always welcome the change and polish this skill to become a versatile , flexible and effective contributor. Because only change is constant and there is always a vacancy at the Top !

Let me take a pause here! ✍

SKILL 13 : TRAVELLING SKILL

PHOTO CREDIT : BARBARA MAIER, UNSPLASH.COM

Hello Friends,

Nice to see on same page !

Friends , we travel often for 'n' no of funny reasons. Sometimes we get homesick and pack our bags , sometimes we receive last minute hint from our superiors for abroad travel with reservation ticket details and we have to on-board within 4-5 hours with cab waiting outside your house . Sometimes , to relax a bit from hard efforts throughout the year , we plan our vacations to some of the exotic global destinations and travel with our loved ones, friends and family ! So, basically travelling is become a vital skill for everybody.

> " We read books to seek knowledge and beauty of thoughtful expressions . We watch TV for funful activities and portray of wonderful characters. We watch movies to experience the best cinematic experience of human emotions packed with descent shoot locations, latest fashion trend and enchanting music . We travel to change our mental atmosphere . We travel to reach newfound destinations to find ourselves .
>
> We travel to breathe in relax mood and gentle feelings. We travel for cause . We travel to cherish relations. We travel to celebrate joy as well as to be a strong beckon of strength in case of pain & sorrows. We travel with travel arrangement which include destination tickets, food & clothes, favorite music & book , the fond companion , if in group – we travel with complete picnic arrangement . Travel offers us beauty of nature , diversity of culture, exposure to social custom & traditions , travel provides you -your space of selfless quest to see the world with open eye and large heart . After every travel ,you will find yourself as a changed mature human being . Travel makes you bold, vigilant and friendly ."

Important steps in attaining travelling skills :

1) Always prefer safe travel.
2) Plan your travel in advance. Intimate location co-coordinators about your arrival and stay arrangements.
3) Ensure right hygiene at stay locations. Be demanding about cleanliness and privacy.
4) Follow crew guidelines and safety instructions whenever they instructs.
5) Carry minimum luggage.
6) For official visit, ensure credit card, mobile SIM and internet connectivity constantly.
7) Get your money exchanged to respective currency in case of international official travel, keep record of your expenses.
8) Be it a water bottle or five star stay, keep bills with you and submit while travel reimbursement claims.
9) Travel at right time. Avoid night times and time during natural calamities whenever possible. In case of urgency, ensure maximum safety.
10) For connecting locations, understand the map with free time. Ensure possible roaming options to pass this time lightly.
11) Ensure enough sleep before and after travel. In travel try to rest yourself in best available ways and postures.
12) Keep your travel document always handy and in safe custody. Take care of your passport and visa.

13) When at different location than your native location, ask for peculiarities of local culture and try to adopt which are possible to you. This helps to gel quickly with locals.
14) Respect other persons time and make sure you finish assigned work in time and also finds yourself free to catch your trip at right time.
15) Indulge in positive meeting outcome and signoff minutes of meeting with all participants.
16) Spread your schedule in such a way that you allow 10 -15% time for situational delays and unexpected events.
17) Make sure, during site visit or shop visit, you take relevant photographs with firms permission to include in your visit report.
18) You are brand representative and hence basic mannerism & custom is an unwritten rule.
19) Explore yourself to nearest destination with local colleague if they request, else ensure you take enough rest.
20) Thanks everybody before your departure and invite them as it find appropriate. Business relations foster with informal bonding and sharing of knowledge with right people.
21) Enjoy your return travel with comfortable sleep.

Hope you liked this chapter. We have tried to explore major aspect of travelling skills.

Let's take a pause here!

SKILL 14 : INFORMATION TECHNOLOGY SKILL

PHOTO CREDIT : ALEJANDRO ESCAMILLA, UNSPLASH.COM

Dear Friends,

Good Evening and nice to see you here !

21st century is best known for computer and information technology boon to mankind with unparalleled growth of the sector in last 20 years. We have seen desktop, floppy drive , pen drive , CD drive, and hard drive and currently we are experiencing the magic of IT with wireless communication technology on our laptop, tablet and mobiles . It's simply stunning and mind blowing . The world has come so much closer and in coming days more and more features will shine this business domain.

> " IT has phenomenal power of connecting mammoth users with simple, safe and open communication channels. IT resolves problems of decision making by adhering to most scientific cognitive approaches . IT has widespread span and its applications are seen in offices, hotels, transport system , personal system , music and sport . It's everybody's favorite technology matter. To unleash the potential of IT , one need to possess the skill of constant learning , one has to be a good programmer and good writer who can co-relate with available parameters easily and effectively !"

A basic course on information technology deals with primary concept about computers , internet and usage of MS office products . Special programming languages help you to master your coding skill to create a best software trail. There is wide emergence of mobile applications , one has to understand these coding languages which allow you to integrate the technology with cross platform modes & mediums. Now-a-days lots of development is happening on machine learning and artificial intelligence technology. One must be conversant with this technical magic.

Let's see which IT skills are necessary as a good professional :

Necessary IT skills :

- Logical thinking and outcome know-how.
- Programming understanding and interface communication basics.
- Customer experience design in case of mobile applications and its optimum usage to get work done through technology.
- Development of software's with the help of observation of physical parameters that can be controlled with the help of software.
- Ability to construct equation with applied work instructions to create systematic MIS to have a bird's eye view of overall work progress.
- Ability to create e-commerce website which will allow connection between suppliers and users to facilitate business transactions.
- Knowledge about IT security system to ensure safe and reliable access to important documents.
- There is emergence of many programming languages, one need to be conversant about their usage as primary programming language or acting as uniform interface.
- Online learning modules to undergo various training to acquire in demand skills and also to carry out bill payment regularly.

- Development as good presenter by using standard presentation templates.
- Showcase your video making skill to create global profile by which you can spread your knowledge with your followers and friends.
- Basic know-how about best communication language , general messaging vocabulary and timing of posts.
- A project report is prepared with large amount of data, reports , tables, images and authorities review. You need to craft out a professional project report by using office soft skills.
- E-mailing is regular activity . You have to master it with frequent precise communication .
- IT is all about systematic tracing of its users. Make sure you use correct privacy setting beforehand to avoid any unwanted attack on your work or your general profile .
- Usage of password and authentication essentials . This skill helps you to protect your data from strangers and attackers, hackers.
- With the use of various blogs and videos posted on internet ,one can easily learn about development in technology . This skill need to be practiced a lot to get fluency .
- Be a good explorer . Develop the habit to ask right question with neat key words.

Hope, you enjoyed this article .

Let's take a pause here!

SKILL 15: MOBILE TECHNOLOGY SKILL

PHOTO CREDIT : MIA BAKER , UNSPLASH.COM

Dear Friends,

Good Evening and welcome again!

In last chapter, we have seen major points about IT skill, with addition to this skill, we are going to see yet another important trending skill of this tech savvy generation –Mobile Technology Skill. Here we will see how mobile has become a one stop solution for all communication, networking and payment needs.

Smart phones has created its important place in the hearts of their users by offering multimedia messaging, number of applications to resolve daily needs, providing instant payment applications to facilitate payment to concern parties. Because of easy accessibility with computers, the pairing with other devices is also become very very easy. This is making data transfer really quick and accurate with all record of file transfer. This has generated great interest in its users and now having mastery in mobile surfing is become a common norm of new generation.

<u>Which are the skills one can learn with mobile? Here is list:</u>

1) *Mobile allows us to connect at any location which makes instantaneous reporting of live issues to arrive at correct decision.*
2) *The data transfer facility with audio, video and image input ,make record available on fingertips which advances decision making.*
3) *We don't need file convertors any more . With online facility we can convert any type of file to other format and get downloaded for free.*
4) *Preparing project report , seminar and technical paper is become a cakewalk . With variety of royalty free stock images one can present the subject in easiest way.*

5) Mobile has huge capacity to store, process and present data. This feature make mobile nearly equivalent to computer.

6) With video conferencing applications, now remote working or working from various locations is become very very simple and it allows seamless connection with all colleagues.

7) With major messaging applications now payment transfer facility is also become very very easy which attracts customer to go for paperless transaction.

8) In coming times with the use of machine learning and artificial intelligence, shopping, networking and informing decision will become very very secure and easy.

9) With the advent of 5G, the speed of internet connectivity will enhance further allowing users to communicate and connect more fast.

10) Data is new fuel and mobile is its reservoir, transmitter & receiver.

With this information one can easily understand the importance of mobile in today's world. However at same time we have to stay away from its harmful effect.

radiation, psychological concerns, care of eye is all major concerns.

As one need to be updated with mobile technology, at the same time one need to be humble, affectionate and courteous in in person dealings. Because personal relation has magic of natural expressions. They are more natural, real and have wonderful gestures.

Earlier facing interview was a big deal as very little information about the organization was available on line. With fast paced growth of web world, every company positioned themselves on digital platform. This help candidate to study company details, know about management and their current achievements, align own knowledge to product delivered by company and think on individual contribution in case asked in the interview. So interview is all about exact presentation of your knowledge with application of practical subject matter. Because of such versatility, mobile is become a great resource of knowledge acquisition.

Friends, we hope you are enjoying these skillful chapters. The aim of our articles is to make you aware, conversant and practical about current employment and entrepreneurial skills in simplest way. We hope, you are practicing these skills to great extent with your friends, study circles and various forums which allow learning these skills faster.Let me allow taking your leave for today. Let's take a pause here!

SKILL 16 : NEWS PAPER READING SKILL

PHOTO CREDIT : MYZINK EGOR, UNSPLASH.COM

Good Morning Friends,

Welcome to interesting chapter of new paper reading skills. Let's start!

We are in a digital edge. We are surrounded ourselves with up to date updates of latest happening in globe on a click or on a fingertip. Whenever we seek information about latest global affairs we surf internet to check the details.

In such a fast paced world, reading the news is become vital to actively stay in touch with environment around us. What would happen if we miss this skill?

The answer is simple. We won't be able to understand effect of changes, decisions and new rules formed and imposed time to time bay various authorities. We will not able to understand the intellectual, logical response generated by social class in response to these new rules or changes. We have to ask each time to somebody about such changes and there is chance that all time we may not be given true input. So, to avoid all these communication and information hurdles, we need to read news and latest happenings consistently.

Reading the newspaper is key skill. Read for headlines, read sport event, read stock markets and material prices, read intellectual & creative thoughts, read brief editorials, read entertainment. A good newspaper has it all!

Read various authors, journalist, specialist, doctors, and scientist! Its club of knowledge bearers. The stories of entrepreneur are always inspiring and it gives practical training to aspirant about the kind of struggle one do while attaining such a bright career.

Why not to read newspaper for? This answer is complex but as we live in large society it is must to present few point which is not necessary to read at all.

One of the subject is events of violence, events of theft and bullying, news that shake personal peace of mind! Such news are present to showcase the other side of society to create awareness about people's incorrect behavior so large mass become aware of such false practices and protect themselves from such social hazards. So such news to be read for general awareness. They are meant for caution.

Interviews are special. They reveal the internal strength, career journey, social status and their opinions on current matters of best achievers. For an aspiring candidate, such reading transfers the confidence level to perform at higher level. Inspirational stories prepare us for crossing untapped potential limits.

In latest technological advances, we are used to read e-paper, e-magazine and e-journals, it's absolutely fine and perfect and we don't need to carry paper with us. But always note, touch with current affairs make our day to day decision making easy.

There was generation of topnotch executives who always start their day by glancing through news of the day. These update in fact used to set their days priority and strategy to deal with any change.

Journalist, editors, distributors and shop sellers put great amount of energy in keeping the fourth pillar of our democracy active and aware. It's our duty to take good out of thousands of event happening in the society.

Benefits of Regular News-Paper Reading:

- You can form your opinion.
- You remain aware, alert and active.
- You get information and hence your decisions tend to be more accurate, precise and time bound.
- You can plan your career choices according to various analytics, surveys & reports shown in the newspaper time to time.
- You get local, national and international understanding of various administrative interaction which help to become a better citizen of the nation.
- Advertisement in newspaper gives information about new products, new services, and new jobs; there is good amount of benefit in interviews when questions on general knowledge are asked by panel.
- A well-read person and a novice can be easily identified with the way of expression of their thoughts during personal interview, which sets selection decision in favor of well-read candidate.
- When you want to improve your communication skill of a particular language, take support of popular newspaper in that language because it has practical language usage which are widely accepted and liked by people.

Let's take a pause here! Hope you liked this! ✍

SKILL 17 : TEAM BUILDING SKILL

PHOTO CREDIT : QUINO AL, UNSPLASH.COM

Dear Friends,

Welcome to this chapter on team building. We will go through wonderful team building details.

> *"Team represents strength, conscience, and unity in diversity, love, care, trust, support. Teams are formedto accomplish missions , to win battles and to achieve cumulative success !"*

When we have to carry out big task, we have to form team of like-minded, qualified, experienced, novice members. Team building starts with team forming which express the purpose of team formation. The mission to achieve the expected goal within given timeframe. While team forming , selection of each member is done with study & review of their unique experience, their skill set , their capability to gel and contribute in team both individually and as a team member . Based on these attributes and depending upon team size which can be micro to macro the team leader forms his team.

Teams can have 2 members, 4 members, 11 members, 50 members or 1000 members. It all depends upon the purpose of team formation, their goals and the different levels of task executing inside team.

Once team is formed, the next step is norming. In this stage, norms are set may be formally or informally. Informal teams have informal norms while formal & professional teams have well written expectation of performance standard. Some norms define what is expected from each team member at certain situation, how team will respond to challenges, how they will maintain unity of thought, action and expressions, how team will contribute to team goal, how mistakes will be nullified in team and how performance will be rewarded in team. This kind of norming is in line with mission and vision of the team. It sets complete team in unison and common ground.

Storming is stage succeeding to norming. In storming, various thoughts, plans and actions are discussed and final understanding is prepared on certain strategies which are necessary to fulfill the goals set. In storming lots of arguments May happen on roles & responsibilities or a concern over typical decision style, but at the end of the meeting team leader and team management has to take a clear call on risks and implications of such bold decisions.

When such think tank is in action, the next path is clear. Hit the ground and win the battle positively. Such battlefield can be a sport ground, seminar-room, office hall or work shop. People gather together, observe the things, collaborate and support each other and complete the goal on victorious note.

As we have in last chapters the role of inspiration and motivation is very very critical in team building. The team leader has to maintain his cool in all situations. The team leader has to be a good listener, open minded, thoughtful, risk taker, action oriented and out of the box player. He has to devise winning strategies, craft out action plan to counter over hurdles and difficulties, he has to act as a compassionate team player to understand some of the unexpected changes that happens during play or work.

When team gets habit of winning on consistent ground, team leader is more than happy to develop the strength, synergy and swiftness of win. Team leader develop new talent, allocate higher responsibilities to senior players and try out new skill building with versatile players. He maintains the momentum of victory and make it regular affair. He builds a fighting spirit with every team member.

However when team faces troubles and defeats , he has to own those defeats and find out the missing performance indicators to correct with enhanced training , changes in roles and all stretch approach to deliver till success and perfection . At times, team leader also has to give ultimatum to non-performing member to ensure he keep his position with improved performance.

A basic professionalism in team behavior ensures total respect, pride and joy with surrounding people. They get energy from such teams and this energy reflects in their performance in respective field.

At the end of the day more than winning the way we win is remembered. A brave hearted loss is always preferable than a victory with cheat and gimmicks. This team spirit of frankness, openness and positivity goes long in building a winning team. When we retire from the game, these are the moments which give us the fond memories and make us playful once again!

Friends, life is a journey of obstacles and chances. We have to surpass obstacles and catch the chances to make our life successful.

We hope you like this. Let's take a pause here! ✍

SKILL 18 :DATA GENERATION SKILL

PHOTO CREDIT :BALAZS KETYI , UNSPLASH.COM

Dear Friends, Good Evening!

Hope you are doing great!

    Earlier before the availability of computers, registers were used to fill up critical details of office work. Be a ledger book or muster for attendance, the record keeping was done with the help of manual paper entry. Off course the work was exhausting, subjected to errors, can have opinion miss-match and number of other issues related to data clarity and retrieval. However some of the oldest system of paper data entry is still working and very very old records are available on request.

> *"With advent of computers and MS Excel set up, onecan easily enter data, save it, copy it, send it, retrieve it, and compare it! This has increased accuracy of data based, well informed decisions. With the optimum usage of various data building software's now record keeping become very very easy and hence time required for reporting is reduced to considerable extent contributing to overall workplace efficiency !"*

But how to develop this necessary advance skill.

Let's see this checklist:

- ✓ Understand the field of study for which you have to collect the data which may be in numbers, currency, quantity or subjective matters.
- ✓ If it is possible to tabularize the data, prepare tables to improve its visibility and finding out interrelation within variables.
- ✓ Data help us to measure frequency of occurrenceof observations. With this frequency, we can keep control on variables.

- ✓ Data is real and the way it is gathered includes sampling, fieldwork and online recording. Hence it stands for accuracy and reliability.
- ✓ Various kinds of data provide us options of decision making. With changes in variables based on trends shown by data, we can forecast or estimate about future trends. This way we can plan our work according to demand estimate to produce sufficient to have expected sales and minimum inventory.
- ✓ As per individual role data can differ in its content. A quality manager has to keep data of no. of customer satisfaction survey while a marketing manager needs to save data of new customer and new territory addition. So based on data type, decision and opinions differ.
- ✓ There are chances that for same work filed two cross functional members can generate miss leading data. Here role of the observer is to test a sample in the field and check the correctness of data. The defaulter has false figures.
- ✓ But how to find out my data is sufficient. Answer is simple. If you can comfortably draw decisions from available data and can decide further steps of work in line with available data, we can say the data is sufficient.
- ✓ Measurement of a pipe dimension includes its OD, ID, Thickness, and Quantity. With these four parameters, thousands of pipes can be measured and separated in typical inventory management

System. When a typical requirement comes, the person sitting at office just glances through master file and communicate its availability with latest price. So he doesn't need to go physically to workstation. This is the power of data generation and data communication.

✓ With latest cloud computing services, we can share any kind of data with decision makers. So we can proceed with crucial decisions accurately

✓ Graphs, Charts and Pyramids need data for their construction. So because of data pictorial understanding of work scenario become simple. In a typical customer pie chart about popularity of brand products, if the data is not available, we cannot draw pie chart to focus our marketing efforts on less selling product or to enhance customer base of high selling product. Thus data make our decisions well informed.

✓ As there are uses of data, there are chances of miss use also. Data can reach to irrelevant person, data can be manipulated, and data can be altered or reduced. Every time sender and receiver has to decide system of checks and balances to ensure data integrity and its optimum usage.

Friends, hope you find this article useful. Data generation is a habit and we need perseverance to generate real, true data. Practice this skill to stay well informed and accurate.

Let's take a pause here!

SKILL 19 : TECHNICAL TRAINING SKILL

PHOTO CREDIT : JESWIN THOMAS, UNSPLASH.COM

Dear Friends,

Welcome to yet another skill building chapter. This skill is technical training skill. This is one of the most sought after and easy skill to develop yourself as in-house authority. Let's go into its details.

Friends, in industry we enter either as trainee or experienced candidate. The first two-three years of career are foundational years and this time is better known for learning basic business practices and technical linkages with business. So getting trained from a reputed in-house trainer is fortunate task and we get good exposure to industrial challenges when we work with good competent trainer with us.

But how to become a good trainer. How to build technical training portfolio and what are benefits of acquiring this skill? Let's see all this through these steps:

Technical Training Skill Development Steps:

1) When we work in a particular domain, we apply our traditional knowledge to find out easy & correct ways of working.
2) As we practice our work, we encounter several challenges and by which we interact with people of different skill sets, experience level and decision making capability.
3) We learn from each other. We learn from mistakes and we learn from system.
4) When this learning phase gets completed, we demonstrate our skills to perform.
5) With increased span of work because of its successful handling, we get conversant with practices and develop our own way of working with efficient implementation of ideas.
6) This sets us apart from people working with us and after some time we get chance to train newcomers entering into organization.

7) When you are working as a trainer, we have to challenge our trainee to think about ways of working, particular status quo andunderstanding of loop holes if present in the system. We have to encourage them to come forward and express their views on ways of working.

8) Before start of training, we have to give brief idea and outline of training. Benefits of training. Provision of certificate if any and we have to ask, what are the changes they would like to implement at work.

9) A competent trainer train according to international curriculum or most preferred content of subject matter. This curriculum may involve quizzes, puzzles, case studies, methods & techniques, mock drills and practical's, presentations and seminars, field work and short term projects.

10) Through such assignments, trainer provides input, assess performance and learning curve and suggest the outcome of training which canbe successful, improvement based or not satisfactory.

11) There is system of repeat exam. Trainer guide to fill up the performance gap. It all depends on commitment of candidate with which he captures and learns these inputs.

12) Once training is completed, the candidate has to implement his learning and provide a project report by using training skills.

13) This report is testimony of his learning and performance improvement at work.
14) With more and more practice, candidate expands his area and achieves success in his domain.
15) Now one of the candidates from such batch of trainees becomes a trainer after few years and this tradition of knowledge transfer continues.
16) Every trainer train about safe working conditions, that is why training is special as it involves hands on experience withunderstanding of risk factors.
17) This way training is different than speech or seminars.
18) Acquired skills boost confidence of both trainer and trainee which in turn improves work force competency and more options of getting work done in challenging situations.
19) A fast growing candidate always prefers to get trained as fast as he can. This adds various skills to his professional experience which helps to perform at higher level.
20) Timely feedback of training builds trust and overall reputation of both trainer and batch he trained.

Friends, hope you find this information useful. Many a time, a self-learning create base for overall development. So always keep learning, experimenting and evolving in life. Let's take a pause here!

SKILL 20 : LEADERSHIP SKILL

PHOTO CREDIT : EVANGELINE SHAW, UNSPLASH.COM

Dear Friends,

Good Evening & welcome to this new chapter!

> " Lead to create new path, lead to read unknown, lead to expand beyond horizon , lead to smile , laugh and enjoy ! Leadership is unique strength ! Live life with a leader's attitude and belief! Never give up!"

In any phase of our life, we learn lots of thing on our own. Sometimes we need instructions while sometime we make our understanding to deal with life situations. The skill of leadership is individual specialty of everyone and as we grow in life we explore all possibilities of our leadership potential.

The path of leader is always a tough road. You have a dream in your mind. You plan your actions. Hurdles meet you during journey. You stop, think, take right action and move ahead towards your path. When you reach desired destination, you enjoy your success along with your followers. This state gives you sense of accomplishment and motivation to do more good for everyone and for yourself.

Leaders have specific traits. Some of them are courage, confidence , clarity , risk taking ability, openness, flexibility, generosity , creativity, negotiation ability, Liaoning ability, quick response to help & support , attention to details as well as relaxation of unnecessary things , leaders are inclusive and they also take firm and strict decisions.

Whenever we search history, we have observed leaders try till end, they may get several failures in their efforts but they again revert with better version of their selves. Leaders know life is a journey; it will have challenges as well as fruits of success. At times, they can wait for result but they also create surprises. They do maintain confidentiality of their work in hand till it gets complete as per their expectation. They believe in perfection and also experimentation.

Success & failure does not alter calmness of leaders mind. Leaders take both these offering equally. Moreover they vanish some failures with their determination, confidence and hard work. Fear is no man's thing for leaders. They are brave and like to associate with brave people.

Leaders possess exceptional integrity and ethics. They are highest morale boosters and they like to talk with compassion and gentleness. Most leaders handle stress with their deep ability to understand root cause of problem and actions to plug those causes.

Leadership position has a specific association of followers which trust and support their leaders. Leaders always have first line, second line strength of followers. These people work with leaders from several years and this brings a human connection of understanding and belief.

For a seasoned leader, developing their followers is a hobby. They never show their insecurity in developing their best supporter and achievers. Loyalty and leadership are big things when issues related to business crisis happen. Leaders move through such challenges with collaborative approach with individual application of field experience and networking ability. Leaders believe in possibilities and they do take chances in which success may not be sure but there is business interest of long term.

Leaders like to love their vision. They are totally committed to their vision. Most of the time, leader coach and consult their team. Ownership is another personal attributes of successful leaders. They do not pass the bucks but they create avenues of clarity and transparency.

Let it be a green field venture or well-established set up, leaders ensure development of humane, interesting and professional system of co-working. They may take help of latest technology, advanced machines and enhanced training module to prepare their staff and associate to make a difference at work consistently.

Ability to reward on special occasion to boost morale of their followers is best attributes of leader. Many a time we have seen, achievers saying, this becomes possible only because of trust put up by leader in initial days. This is charm of a leader. They develop their followers along with their own growth. Rather growth of followers is real indicator of a leader's charisma. Leaders create leaders for future generations that are what success of leaders generally counted.

Friends, hope you enjoyed this chapter. Be a leader, be an achiever of your life! Let's pause here!

SKILL 21 : CREATIVE SKILL

PHOTO CREDIT : AAAAAAAAAAAAAA, UNSPLASH.COM

Good Morning Friends,

Wish you a bright morning and bright thoughts here!

> *"Creativity creates wonderful power of imagination. It is different eye of looking at things. It adds beauty, purpose and rhythm to ones thinking pattern!"*

Ability to design something is result of knowledge, ideas, skill and artistic thinking. Knowledge takes care of structure of the unit, idea look after the ingenuity and uniqueness, skill makes work fast irrespective of hurdles in implementation of ideas and artistic thinking combine the best possible options of artistic feel in the form of size, shape and colour of the object.

Who are creative people? Let's list out!

List of creative people:

1) All artists are creative people. They explore bright ideas. Out of several ideas presented in front of people, several ideas are liked & loved by people and this pave path of success to creative people. Inclination, interest and imaginations stand true in success of popular artist.

2) All Engineering designers are creative people. They draft out different drawings of industrial parts to provide products with ease of manufacturing, scalability, fitness for intended purpose, estimated budget and cost effectiveness and easiest portability. They have to apply their knowledge, skill & experience to design their product out of nothing or on the basis of proven or unproven scientific principles to shape their ideas into a feasible commercial solution. The extent of technical produce determines ultimate success of their design.

3) Scientist and research scholars are highly creative people. They dig deep into knowledge domain of unknown with their unparalleled curiosity, constant zeal to understand the complexity of the challenges and referencing habit to grasp the knowledge to arrive at a particular innovation. Every innovation has some base of past achievement and past technological model. Means the discovery of electric bulb is a major invention but creation of LED bulb is innovation. Here discovery of electricity bulb is happened out of thousand unsuccessful attempts of its generation, while innovation of LED bulb may not be that long. They checked possibility of applying LED principles to existing design of bulb; they replaced filament wire with LED light source. Earlier heat of filament wire with the help of power of reflection possessed by glass is used to generate light source while now power of light emitting diode along with reflective power of white colour or other colors is used to create light source of different colors. Also they provided main focus on less electricity consumption which becomes a commercial attraction and way of instant success. This is what creativity all about. When an idea clicks, it become popular and gives prestige, fame and money. This is proven creativity indeed! In future some more development will happen to provide this innovation more easily.

4) Every technician and workmen is a master creator. They do the practical task of conversion of ideas into reality. How many of us know that a typical circular shape shown on the drawing of a metallic part, takes number of hours in practical world of manufacturing. If we take example of casting , designer will provide the drawing but process metallurgist has to think on mold design, arrangement of risers & gaters, direction of metal flow, way of solidification of metal to ensure uniform cooling across its thickness, metal pouring characteristics and adherence to its composition , possibility of failures in case of issues during melting , pouring and solidification, necessary adjustments in parameters to ensure a product with right quality , right mechanical properties and right scalability. Then come success!

5) Creative people are practical thinkers; they know what is possible and how the things can be developed in best possible way. They are self-starters and driven by their passion to create new stuff always!

Friends, let's take a pause here! We hope, with this article you may have understand the fundamental advantage of being creative! Creativity sets you apart from the rest of the crowd and it makes your unique identity.

SKILL 22 : MEETING & DISCUSSION SKILL

PHOTO CREDIT : CHERRYDECK, UNSPLASH.COM

Good Morning Friends,

Welcome to this chapter of meeting and discussion skill. Let's see essentials points of this skill.

Friends, meetings are integral part of one's professional life. When we work together, we have separate and combined task to complete. We need uniform, right and fast direction. This is achieved by meeting with responsible stakeholders. Meetings are one of the most popular forms of problem resolution.

Naturally meetings are followed by discussions to arrive at required decision of team, necessary sharing of responsibility, addressing the changed way of working or it can be celebration of achievement of annual performance. Let's see how meetings are conducted and how decisions are taken.

General way of conducting meetings:

A. The chairperson calls for meeting which is supported by meeting co-coordinator to discuss inform and act on subject under discussion.
B. The chairperson can be a team leader, department head or captain of the team. They unite people at one location.
C. When people come, the agenda of meeting is put forward and meeting gets started.
D. People present their concern, opinions, action plan and ideas on subject matter.
E. These points are brainstormed to find out a best possible solution.
F. In meeting there can be disagreement over few issues for which more meetings are organized after certain interval and resolution of concerns.
G. There are some common practices in interacting in meeting. Everybody get their turn to present their opinion hence its best to prepare for putting good ideas and points. Accept good suggestions of others

and talk friendly in case of any disagreements. Adhere to meeting time and other urgencies. Meeting needs to be concise, clear and to the point. Make sure you note minutes of the meeting when meeting is going on. These minutes can be send to participant as arecord and for future usage.

H. Meetings can be held at ground as in sports before start of the match, in office or in shops.

I. Shop meeting are related to concerns related to way of working, sharing of change in method and addressing common administrative notifications.

J. Meetings can happen with cross functional as well as remote located team members to share status of various happening, preparation at their end and to provide further plan of action.

K. Frequency is important concern in scheduling meetings. Please note, everybody has equal time and their duties and by sparing or allocating time from these activities, one has to arrive for meeting. So no of meetings should be enough to present the point quickly and effectively. Generally meeting are conducted at the start of the day for 15-20 minutes, at the end of the day for 10-15 minutes to understand days progress, once in a week, month or quarter to review set performance standards and to bridge gap with any shortfalls, annual meeting are large scale affair and it may involve call to all stakeholders, shareholders and all related people.

L. We have to be neat, clean and presentable in

meeting. Our expressions should be logical and we should answer tactfully to ensure our arguments are logical and result oriented. Vague arguments in meeting wastes time and resolve nothing.

M. When in doubt, it's always better to wait until the person finishes their sentence and then we can ask politely about our doubt or concern. This helps the speaker to understand the concern and suggest his opinion on that doubt. Stopping in between create chaos and waste time.

N. It's not possible to have all answers available all time. Take time to answer and tell them to contact in person with detailed information.

O. Meetings become effective with presentation. So, when you are main speaker in meeting, it's always better to prepare a short hand presentation of bullet points, current status and projected status.

P. Some of the meeting ends on lighter notes with snacks & tea. Be participative and enjoy informal networking happens in the meeting. It helps to build understanding.

Friends, lets pause here! We hope, we have talked and noted general meeting skills here!

Decisions are outcome of meeting; hence we should always try to have our meeting result oriented.

SKILL 23 : PRESENTATION SKILL

PHOTO CREDIT : CAMPAIGN CREATORS, UNSPLASH.COM

Hello Friends,

Welcome to this chapter of presentation skill!

> *"Presentations are simple arrangement of facts, data, trends, analysis and concerns to provide general awareness. Presentation provides knowledge, clarity and confidence to its viewers. Presentations also has fun and curiosity element!"*

How to create successful presentations:

- Choose the topic of presentation.
- Explore information about the topic in detail.
- Detail includes history, development and current status of presentation topic.
- Systematic presentation understands quickly hence try to be in order when presenting.
- If you are presenting without power point presentation feature, make sure you talk confidently and you take people in confidence. This can be done by asking engaging questions, starting mindful activities such as asking about general idea of topic, awareness about latest happening in this topic, work out some fun drills to make audience active and interested.
- When you are presenting with power point presentation, include pictorial slides with diagrams, pictures and animations. Take care you keep the right quantum. Too many animations are not suggested. Slides should be self-explanatory and you should talk for at least aminute per slide.
- Generally slides include synopsis of point of discussion, so points should be bulleted and highlighted.
- Transition period and transition style should be relatable; it depends on topic of presentation. When we are presenting technical presentation, we can go with easy to read & understand slide design, when we are presenting entertaining

- presentation, the slide design need to be attractive, funful and fresh.
- Time of presentation is important aspect. General professional presentation span up to 30 minute-45 minute. Seminars and round table conferences can have 3-4 hours of presentations of unique presenter with 1 or 2 breaks in between. Speech is also a presentation of thought, opinion and ideas, it generally last for half hour to one hour.
- A successful presenter always knows their audience and take care that he is audible, presentable and lively during presentation.
- Presentation needs to be distraction free and hence presenter requests their audience to switch off mobile and cherish silence for effective presentation.
- In case of disturbances or uncomfortable moments during presentation, take a glass of water; wait for some time, request audience to maintain decorum. People do listen.
- At the end of the presentation ask for any queries or questions. It's a good gesture to go for it.
- Answer the question with your understanding of the subject. This reveals your depth of knowledge.
- If you don't know few answers, make sure you provide your contact details in the end of the presentation, try to contact person who ask query for its timely resolution. Time can be 1 day to 3 day.
- Laser beam Pointers are used to focus on presentation points, use it often.

- Also provide notepads and pens to people to capture important points if they wish. This depends on the size of audience. Currently because of smartphone one can actually record the live presentation and then store or save in their system for future study & reference.
- You should be aware about set up of projector, laptop and sitting arrangement. Make sure you stand straight, with positive body language and at central location.
- Presentation is all about managing time, in tricky situations of fumble during activity such as not remembering the content, too much questions and doubts, slides are not understood by audience, relax a bit and listen to people queries. Your ability to connect with audience in logical ways resolves such tricky situation.
- Thanks audience for their patient listening and active involvement.
- Take descent feedback about presentation for further improvement. As learning is a lifelong process.

Friends, hope you find this article helpful. Practice thisskill regularly to become a master presenter.

Let's take a pause here!

SKILL 24 : DEVILS ADVOCATE SKILL

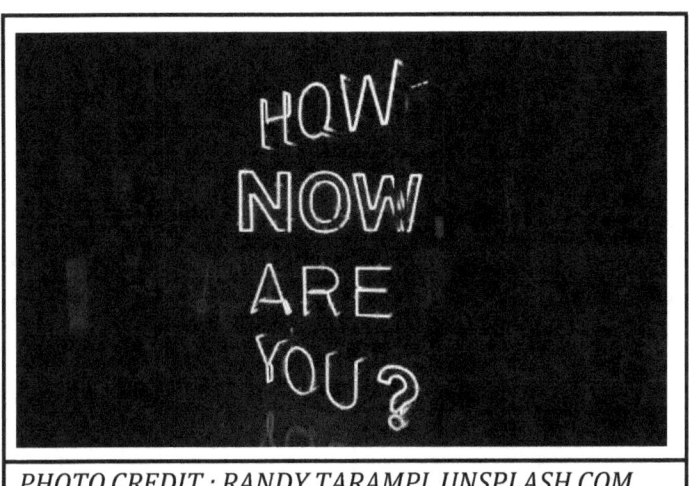

PHOTO CREDIT : RANDY TARAMPI, UNSPLASH.COM

Good Morning Dear Friends,

Welcome to this skill chapter – Devil's Advocate Skill!

Sounds strange but this is one of the special skill we need to acquire in our career or in personal life. Advocacy is basically about thinking in all both directions, right and wrong. When we think in right direction, we apply our logic to devise a way of its implementation. We develop plans, take actions, observed results and quantify our achievement. With review of our result we become happy and content. This is an ideal case scenario.

In reality, while dealing with situations we encounter several unexpected hurdles. These hurdles disturb our normal plan of action and consume our useful time in their association. They reduce our efficiency and make things difficult for us to achieve quickly.

> *"Here comes the role of devil's advocate . Devil's advocate is way of inclusive thinking which takes into account kind of hurdles those can arise during execution of our planned activity and to decide our plan of action to counterbalance and win over those hurdles. In this way, devil's advocate in fact ensures safety of your result by proactively thinking and mitigating the risks associated with careless execution! Devil's advocate is about thinking what could go wrong and what can be outcomes of such events and our response. Probability of happening of such event is very very low but when it happens, it costs a lot! So it's always important to safeguard our interest by thinking proactively, constructively and logically about adversities . This is known as devil's advocate!"*

Some of the examples of planning for adversities:

1) Financial stability is one of the important aspects of any business. Business experience cycles of variation of demands. In such situations, to avoid inventory stack up and associated dead costs one has to plan for optimum production capacity. This is done by producing more in less time by which cost of manufacturing come down. Same thing happens with overhead cost. With the help of cost cutting, cost saving and strict budgeting one can ensure business sustenance in adverse situation. When there is huge demand, we add resources to make production feasible, but when there is slowdown, these overheads increase. In such cases hiring multi skilled manpower become useful as these people can work at different locations. So if business has several functions, we can appoint this excess manpower at different location. So when sudden slowdown or loss happens, business takes care of survival package through its previous provisions.

2) You are visiting a remote site for 4 day and it may happen that your stay may prolong for two more days, in such a case, you reserve tickets for two possible departures. In case you manage your work within time you cancel second one. In case you extend your work, you cancel your first ticket. Off course cancellations has cost but they are always lesser than emergency tickets and their availability. This way proactively you take

care of event in which you need to extend your work beyond schedule.

3) Business expansion happens with various site survey and proximity to customer base and natural resources. A businessman has to think in advance for choice of possible location. During initial stages, they talk with various state governments about business startup in their states. If the business policy of state is ensuring peace, descent tax rate and resource availability, they prefer that state as it ensure their profitability in both short & long term. But suppose a state do not allow or put up heavy taxes, business has to think for second option in safe zone. This way they manage their dependence on one state to have freedom of their choice. Many times government also support businesses by making laws promoting entrepreneurial culture which may involve faster processing, tax holidays and concessional offers of land purchase . So choice is always there to plan for business adversities.

Hope you find this chapter and information useful. Plan for adversities and stay secure in crisis, this is what devil's advocate is all about!

Let's take a pause here!

SKILL 25 : AUDITING SKILL

PHOTO CREDIT : VIKTOR TALASHUK , UNSPLASH.COM

Good Afternoon Friends,

Welcome to this chapter of Auditing skills.

When we are delivering a product or service to large number of customers with commercial price, customer expect to receive every product with exactly same features for a typical price band. This uniformity is achieved by its manufacturer by way of standardization its manufacturing quality system and safety system of its complete environment. System has vision, mission, operations, roles, responsibilities, process, work instruction, non-conformances, certifications, approvals, acceptances, rejections. Because of this standardization one can ensure product of particular batch details has certain properties because during their realization record of same is kept at factory end. So when they certify about product features, means they have tested and approved before sending it to market ensuring quality and safety of their product and people using it!

How this uniformity is achieved? The answer is sophisticated machines and skilled, qualified manpower. Machine knows its mechanism of creation while operators know machine functioning. Operators observes whether machine is doing correct things while supervisors observe whether operators and machine encounter any operational , technical, material, maintenance issue . To finance and support for supervisors challenges there is system of management which coach and resolve capital expenditure, vision and mission implementation challenges. Beyond shop management there is board of directors which take care of customers and investors interest by addressing annual business performance ensuring customer satisfaction and business profitability which can provide decent return on investment to its stakeholder. People investing in shares study business trends and invest or withdraw their investment to keep their investments safe all time.

Up & down in the business because of demand-supply, price-profit, and competition – new product entry causes shift in investor's preferences. Board has to take care of investors' interest for long term.

> *" Here comes the system of audit into picture ! With predefined intervals of internal & external audits as per the specific certification requirement , organization has to develop internal auditors which carry out internal audits of their cross functional processes, department heads and present their observations, findings and non-conformances and approvals of their audit report. Auditee has to resolve issues noted during audit by applying preventive and corrective action plan , sharing to all stakeholders and keeping regular records of updates in system manual with all amendment details . This way increases transparency of system and processes ensuring achievement of required quality , quantity and business turnover !"*

This way audits are health card of your quality and safety management system. There is specific training programme to become an auditor. In this training, details about conducting audits, planning audits, closing audits is taught with some of the specific case studies and audit trails. Audit is conducted with documented proof of records, so there is no chance of changes in record. This way audit reflects the regular way of working of particular system. An audit report without any non-conformances and recommendation for re-approval is what every manufacturer expects fromhis team!

Let's take an example of audit finding.

In a purchase audit involving high value transaction , following documents are reviewed – Purchase order, part drawing , supplier approval record, part receipt invoice and goods received note,inspection report from supplier and in house check of item, issue record of item and its balance stock in store . Consumption record in shop and its allocation to specific serial no of production. Review of test certificate in which respective part is fitted and its customer details. Record of any complaint received on part supplied as well as any appreciation letter shown by department head when asked by auditor. This way auditor ensures all round cross checks of particular transactions.

Friends, hope you find this information useful. It requires sound experience of cross functional working before becoming an auditor. Audit report need to be clear, specific and in order mentioning observations with their supporting evidences. This make audit report actionable and reliable. Let's take a pause here! ✍

SKILL 26 : REPORTING SKILL

PHOTO CREDIT : DISRUPTIVO. UNSPLASH.COM

Good Evening Friends,

Welcome to new chapter, reporting skill.

Reporting is important part of job life and business dealings as well as personal life! Reporting is communication of status to reporting authority that reviews your performance and help to shape up your career. Everybody has designated role in organization and everybody has an assigned reporting authority. Various types of approvals are authorized to your reporting authority which includes approval of allocated responsibility, signing authority and transaction limit, authority to approve leave, authority to recommend for training, authority to recommend for promotion.

Success in career is mostly depends on one's individual performance but at the same time right guidance, direction and feedbacks received from your seniors. When you are new into office, your timely reporting and completion of task help to create your identity. Depending upon your actions, authorities offer you various new roles which justify your talent and make you independent at earliest to develop as major contributor.

Initially you need to report frequently as your decision making skills are not developed, there are chances of practical error, the issues you tackle could have deeper technical complexity and commercial implications, to make your road smooth, you always need to have habit of regular reporting. On communication of current status and if there are any challenges, your supervisors intervene to set your rapport with colleagues, make you comfortable with good engineering practices and culture of the organization because of which you blend with them to perform with speed and accuracy . This increases your public acceptance and after that you start taking your decisions. With this development you report results as you are aware about common way of working.

This stage in career increase your trust level with seniors and they become more open with you suggesting development of your talent in business need and your personal choice . Many a times, the thinking of seniors and your preference may not match, but it's your ability to learn & grasp the things make you winner in challenges faced by you.

Let's point out reporting essentials:

1. Seek time for regular meeting.
2. Discuss the project progress.
3. Identify critical steps of your duty.
4. Suggest your innovative ideas to make work easy a simple.
5. Communicate true status. Incomplete task can be completed with proper communication.
6. Adhere to major timelines. Seniors loves exceeding target with precision and regularity.
7. Speak up for your doubts, queries and hurdles. An open communication helps to establish co-operation and long term engagement.
8. Generate monthly MIS; it helps to set transparency of your performance and easy way to have guidance on achievements and improvements.
9. When you are managing a team, report to your senior about team's progress. Discuss the individual potential and craft out training plan

with approval of your seniors. Here you act as representative of middle management.

10. Performance at work for a manager is result of active participation of all team members. However on practical ground, everybody can't perform to their potential. There are various issues of adjustment, role clarity, knowledge gap, motivation, different insecurities. With the help of constant reporting changes in behavior can be achieved. Here you constantly encourage your colleague to learn work, take tactful decisions, record your way of working and thus monitor your own performance over time to find development happened.

11. Rewards and recognition happen with acceptance of your performance. In case you not achieve your recognition, talk to your reporting authorities for specific improvement points.

12. Know your strengths and weaknesses and always thrive to become a quick learner and logical decision maker. This will create your identity as serious player.

Friends, we have seen many colleagues who stay more than 20 years together in same organization. Reporting of such colleagues is mere matter of trust. The way we discuss in our family, same is the case when we work with same superiors for number of years together. You both help to contribute to individual progress and role success. Hope you liked this chapter.

Let's take a pause here! ✍

SKILL 27 : WORK-LIFE BALANCE SKILL

PHOTO CREDIT : HYBRID, UNSPLASH.COM

Good Morning Friends, Hope you are doing great!

Childhood is such an affectionate affair. Its time of genuine joy, new learning's, playfulness and exploring ourselves in unknown direction with lovely guidance, support and encouragement from our parents, teachers, friends and society. We pass an age of formal communication in which we acquire knowledge, acceptable public behavior skill and academic success with the help of constant efforts put in our studies.

The age in which we study is one of the delicate ages of human life. In this age we are surrounded with all kind of attractions and it is very very difficult to concentrate on one particular thing. So success earned in studies is sample of what we can achieve in our life ahead. This may not be true for everybody, there may be exceptions but on gross scale, academic success stand as entry ticket for business success.

When we enter this sector either as employee or as individual owner of family run business, we have lots of aspirations, goals and dreams. We are now in a different world. This world works hard, party hard and learns soft! This world sets huge targets and achieves it with shear passion and determination. This world share knowledge with constructive co-working and surpass expectations by continuously upgrading their performance and portfolio. Ultimately , we also feels , we should have distinct achievement , unique identity and all true success measures with us in this family of professionals and entrepreneurs.

To make our dream true, we fulfill and deliver our duties and responsibilities and get appropriate rewards for our contribution. As we progress in our career different life events happen which includes confirmation in service or establishment of business, salary rise or growth in customers, confirmation in service or tie up with big associations to become part of big successful family, marriage , kids and their education and upbringing and their career. By this time we reach an age where we find we are completely stuck in environment of standard duty hours and almost become monotonous for last 20-25 years. We get a feeling of boredom and we find our ways of adhering to work-life balance to keep us healthy, funful and active at the age of above 30. But what will happen if we balance of work and life from day one of our office joining. It will simply set our life in order and make us feel happy of any transformations in our life. Friends, let's see how this work-life balance is achieved from start of professional life!

Work –Life Balance Principles from Day 1:

1) Respect time and become a winner!
2) Start early, may be 15 minutes before the time to feel relax, quiet and confident.
3) Learn to adopt switch on and switch off practice of mental baggage. Do work in office and relax in home.
4) Always discuss your concern with your team and try to develop common notions of performance. Understand strength and weaknesses of everybody and fill up the gap with your skills to perform as a cohesive team.
5) Team working has several advantage, if team wins, everybody wins, if team loose, generally captain accept the responsibility but non-performer also has to pay price. So work with

100% dedication to meet your target consistently.

6) It is always good to practice our skills in initial phase of career. Harder the efforts you put in your career in early days, simpler is your understanding of basic fundamentals and business concept.

7) Cherish a hobby, be a part of cultural group and achieve excellence in your hobby, perform in front of your friends and creative circles and enjoy the atmosphere!

8) Associate with sports! Sports keep you active, positive and healthy. Sports boost up your stamina and 'never say die 'attitude. Sports offer flexibility of attitude and keep you're grounded in moments of win & loss. Sport encourages you to do better in every new attempt.

9) Earn honestly, spend wisely, invest correctly and secure firmly to ensure healthy financial status of all time!

10) Make friends and network often. Share your knowledge, skill and achievement in your professional circles and participate in various social events organized by these professional bodies.

11) Learn the purpose of life; keep your life worthy and happy for you. This is little facts of a proper work –life balance. Hope you like it!

Let's take a pause here!

SKILL 28 : PROFITABILITY SKILL

PHOTO CREDIT : RUPIXEN, UNSPLASH.COM

Dear Friends,

Good morning & Welcome to this chapter of profitability!

Education has the power of spreading light of knowledge with all same time. Its individual capacity to grasp this knowledge, apply at right location at right time and become a winner of life! We see many people struggling in their life because of lack of education.

Business has very very strong foundation of education. Scientist study nature , natural phenomenon, invent their ideas , shape up these ideas in a practical product and showcase and sell it to society for betterment of their material life !

Spiritual Teachers taught us the ultimate purpose of our life and suggest the importance of hard work, honesty, determination, openness, kindness in our spiritual life. This life is all about values and principles. This teaching help us to know ourselves better to understand true meaning of life which is serving the society with all good deeds to achieve ultimate satisfaction and peace of mind!

Then why this chapter of profitability? Friends, to buy material things earlier we have system of barter and exchange. As time evolved, we come up with currency system which is unified way of purchase of any material thing. As world is huge and has many countries, everyone developed their own currency. Nations have resources and other nations need those resources. People fought wars to protect their territory of these resources by keeping statesman united, strong and alert. In a civilized society, material transactions happened with exchange of resources on the basis on international benchmarking of material price according to its quality and importance.

Work hard, create product, sell those product to consumers, customers at a price reasonable acceptable to you and your consumer, subtract production cost, overheads and taxes and keep your balance earning as your profit! This is the central theme of business and profitability.

On prima facie, it looks very very simple but it's not that easy. Making constant profit out of your business activity is all about establishing business that caters to people dire need , create products or services which satisfy those need, let people like your offering and regularly purchase it, set a price which take care of your production cost and peoples general earning potential , market your offerings in clear, useful and attractive ways , inform people about benefits of your product , keep your product ahead of several players in competitive market , win the price or quantity war , cherish your customers and offer new products ,adjust to various laws and amendments enforced from time to time , accept up and downs of business demand cycles, reward & compensate fairly to people working with you , have latest technology and machines to keep your production cost less and create in abundance whenever situation occurs , from all such mammoth measures you ensure profitability of your business.

When you earn a certain profit, invest it to expand your business, this will increase your sales by which you further earn more profit. With changing time, you will find another sector in which you can excel and you start investment in that sector. With building robust system with qualified manpower and other resources, you set this business segment also and start earning profit. More and more people join you and they start contributing and developing their selves into a healthy professional environment. You ensure equal opportunity to everybody by planning their professional lifecycle which involve their timely promotions, salary rise and sense of attachment with you! Same people for considerable amount of time develop confidence in team and team achieves difficult goals with shared vision and perfect missions. Not everybody is equal but unity makes things profitable.

> " Price – Cost = Profit is most famous and simple profit formula. With increased competition, you either need to have a very very demanding product of regular use or you need to create products which are a skill par excellence and used in very very special purpose. Now if you prepare such precious product with least cost, you increase chances of profitability. Material strength should never be compromised as it stands as identity of your product. Your product has number of features but if it is not durable, people will switch to more durable product at increased price which will give advantage of better quality to your competitors. So you have to make superb product, market them and sell them constantly to book profits!"

Friends, we hope you liked these concepts. Constantly update yourself to develop business centric social products to ensure profitability. Let's pause here! ✍

SKILL 29 : VOCABULARY BUILDING SKILL

PHOTO CREDIT : SIGMUND, UNSPLASH.COM

Dear Friends,

Welcome to new chapter of skill development. Let us see more about vocabulary building skill.

> " *Language speaks emotions. Emotion express person. Person meets each other. Person work together . Person prospers together. All it startswith an electric smile and gentle words - Hello ,How are you ?"*

As we have seen earlier, English is widely accepted as a formal business language and so speakers of this language has international scope and progress path open in all directions. For native English speakers it's almost natural to speak in this language as it is their mother tongue. Novice finds it challenging to speak in this language because of various pronunciation aspects, tact's of understanding syntax and grammar of this beautiful language. The environment in which they live may not use this language as first and preferred language of communication.

Mastery over language is a skill of practice. You need to think in this language, then you have to write in this language, slowly you have to increase your friend circle which practices this language during their formal-informal communication, you have to arrange discussions on various topics and should provide a chance to come front and speak with confidence .When you speak, you get feedback about your expressions. Some may like it, some may give you feedback, and some will suggest certain errors or tell you about usage of particular word. This way you will get ample scope for practicing this language.

When it's about language, it's about grammar and words. As grammar has limited content to study with parts of speech, words are endless. Without mastery in grammar, you cannot remember the words and their meaning. We know similar words, opposite word, adjective, noun, verb, and adverb, tense. We have

Lots of options available to decide the style of our communication with other to attract or distract. Its game of words, grammar and tense. But always remember, language becomes our first identity and understanding of our emotional intelligence. A soft spoken bunch of words create feeling of confidence, trust and support with each other while a series of harsh words hurts people . Yes it really hurts and people tend to react in similar fashion with you.

Some considerate people will understand you and talk with improvement suggestion. These suggestions are about improving our vocabulary. Let's see how vocabulary is improved.

Vocabulary Improvement Skill:

- Practice new words with their spelling, pronunciation, meaning and usage.
- With taking one word for day, at the end of year you will have 365 words fully remembered and fully understood.
- Once you are confident about their usage, use gently in typical communication set up. When you introduce a new word in the communication channel, people look and understand you as expert of that language and converse with you which again increase your interaction skill.
- Try speaking for long intervals in front of mirrors; this gives idea about how you look in front of people while speaking. Always remember when you are fluent with language;

you speak confidently, clearly and concisely.

- For new practical words magazines, novels and movies are great resource. They also show native pronunciation of words usage.
- Too much difficult words which are not generally used may be noted for knowledge but the basic words commanding salutation, respect, permission, approvals should be remembered without fail.
- There are English proficiency exams based on your verbal, written and comprehension skill. Try to pass & excel in those exams.
- Plays are real time events of language understanding participate in such play and polish your skills.
- Newspaper and editorials has lots of important words. Make it habit to read newspaper often.
- In various networking platform, you may make new friends and can start actual conversation. This gives a big boost to learn the language quickly, at the same time you can both each other native language, and it's so simple and beneficial to understand the beauty of language skills.
- Keep your brain active by solving word puzzles. This is trickiest way to improve vocabulary.
- Love language to live in that language!

Hope you find this information useful.

Let's pause here!

SKILL 30 : SUPERVISION SKILL

PHOTO CREDIT : GEX XAVIER, UNSPLASH.COM

Dear Friends,

Good afternoon and welcome to this chapter of supervisory skills. This chapter will express various aspects of industrial supervision along with real life examples. It will add to your knowledge kitty fundamental principles of supervision. It will explain how efficiency and effectiveness is improved by different trick of supervision. Finally we will see people skill of a good supervisor.

1) Imagine a class of sixty students withoutavailability of teacher!
2) Imagine class of student without an examiner.
3) Imagine class of same students working in organization without a supervisor.
4) Imagine class of same students felicitated by all industry experts for their contribution to technical field without any guidance.

Is this possible right now?

Has it happened anywhere recently that a certain group learns, do and excel in all things without any support, guidance,direction, evaluation.

Is educational automation tried anywhere, in which student will come to school, learn all the things on their own and excel without any examination!

Can this possible?May be!

But, Supervision is necessary to certify, validate and publish your learning potential which ultimately decides the way of your earning, your customer portfolio and the extent of your earningpotential.

Self-certification may not!"

Supervision in industrial environment is about front facing team of professionals who deals with workmen and operators as well as cross functional management professionals working in the field. Supervisors are single point contact about communication from management to workmen & operators about production target , welfare policies, duty norms , leave & attendance management , conflict reporting , maintenance reporting, material requisition , skill development and training , health and safety assessment of environment and first hand contact in case of emergency situations happened in shop floors.

Supervisors are mainly responsible and accountable of timely production and realization of maximum work orders by adhering to system norms and by improving work environment by devising simple ways of working, by improving team morale, by implementing various incentive schemes for performance boost, by carrying out cleanliness and easy accessibility projects for machine and shop floor.

They have to look after secure storage, usage and disposal of material coming to their stockyard. Any loss of property has to take care by constant vigilance and appropriate controlling measures to safeguard organizations property.

They have to train new workmen by arranging in house or external training programmes. They have to educate workmen for practicing safe working conditions at work and have to encourage in escalating unsafe practices immediately. They need to study the drawings in detail for successful manufacturing of items. They have to seek co-ordination and support of various service functions like maintenance, quality, and administration for getting respective work done.

Many a times during various demands from workmen and operators, they have to represent management as right, firm and clear demonstrator of Organizations policy. To improve effectiveness and efficiency they constantly monitor work in progress and suggest corrective actions immediately. They take care of tool cribs and ensure required tools and tackles are available for everybody. People skill including confirm attitude, right direction, accurate pairing and team building, mutual trust and co-operation enhancement these tasks also a part of supervision.

To respond to follow up from management they have to update the status of work by ways of productions trackers and visual management of workplace .During audit, they have to show evidences of material transaction, production and issues reported on quality and safe working conditions.

Its foundation role for becoming industrial leader. Lots of chief executives spend considerable time of their career while serving for shop floor actively during their initial period of service. Hope you find this chapter useful.

Let's take a pause here!

SKILL 31: MANAGERIAL SKILL

PHOTO CREDIT : AUSTIN DISTEL, UNSPLASH.COM

Dear Friends,

Welcome to the chapter –Managerial Skill!

> *" Ability to manage situations is effect of planning, co- ordination, control and leading . The person with these qualities becomes a successful manager in course of time !"*

Let's see this imaginary story to understand various aspects of managerial skills:

Mr. Frank is CEO of a mid-size manufacturing organization with annual turnover about 20 CR with team of 70 workmen. This organization manufacturer's structural items which are supplied to various customers at their site for civil foundations. Mr. Frank runs a private organization now and planning to go public within next five years when their annual turnover reaches 75 CR with total manpower 250.

Mr. Frank is supported by team of sales & marketing professionals, production manager, material manager, quality manager, human resources manager. They have ISO 9001: 2015 quality certification and also hold ISO 14000 HSE certifications.

Addition to 70 workmen, Mr. Frank is supported by 25 junior staff in various business functions. Everybody has appraisal measures and full team works in total unison.

At the start of the month Mr. Frank organize a meeting with their core team about orders in hand, priorities, advance and balance of payment status, funds availability for next month's operation and this month's fund availability status. It is habit of Mr. Frank to plan for one month's advance liquidity to ensure seamless production. This habit is cherished since last 3 years.

Planning of material happen in same week and all necessary raw materials is procured with 75%

upfront payment and balance 25% with credit period of 120 days. This strategy helps Mr. Frank to procure enough material as per their requirement. They have tie up with channel partners of major mills supplying this raw material. Two partners are their college friends.

Mr. Frank has a dedicated placement agency for recruitment of non-technical staff and contract labour which look after manpower requirement. Permanent staff is managed by human resource and they prefer only local candidate with 50-50 gender equality ratio.

Be it a man or women , Mr. Frank arranges training programmes of skill development because of which their staff feel motivated, charged and confident to handle challenges. Appraisal and promotions happen with regular interval and Mr. Frank provided basic facilities in comparable amount to keep employee happy and performing.

From second week of every month to third week of every month, Mr. Frank along with their production, quality and material manager together review the status of plan and make decision of final monthly targets. Before start of last week, with available man-hour's calculation and receipt of payment and order follow up status, they adjust priority of deliveries to ensure payment from customers before end of the next month. They give 90 days' credit period to customers with 30 % advance, 45% on finished good condition and 25% after successful errection from their site people.

Mr. Frank has market reputation of fastest 1000 installation of structures at various civil construction sites. This reputation ensures payment within completion of credit period mostly within 15 days of finished good. This is track record of their service team.

Mr. Frank being MS from reputed foreign university relies heavily on advanced technology in manufacturing and insists their staff to learn advancement in joining methods. They just implemented a training programme in which they certified 10 new TIG welder and 10 GMAW welders.

Since the complete workshop is located nearby a village which is away from city mere 15 KM, there is ample availability of storage place for finished goods and hence they have made temporary shade for such storage. Their workshop host 10 jobs at one time and it operate in two shifts. The shift communication is done by dedicated software and there is 100 % clarity about work completion and work balance.

People are conscious about quality and they ensure more than 95% accurate work with minimum rework suggested by their quality executives and managers. They also have special distinction of 1000 accident free day!

Mr. Frank encourages team to participate in social event and insist to have one weekly off compulsory. We hope, you would like to work with Mr. Frank, frankly! Let's pause here!

SKILL 32: BRAND AMBASSADOR SKILL

PHOTO CREDIT : HELLO I'M NIK, UNSPLASH.COM

Hello Friends, Good evening and welcome to the new chapter – Brand Ambassador!

> *"Brands are built with lots of hard work and patience. Reputation of brand stands for identity and performance of their product and services. Hence person showcasing for these brands is meant to possess same or similar qualities, achievements and ethics!"*

Brand Stories & Brand Ambassadors:

1) A children's favorite nutritional product brand select youngest under 19 champion sportsman to promote their brand. Here benefits of brand can be well experienced by person who is endorsing it! Everybody likes to become like this sportsman, they try this brand and when they like its quality and test, they choose to continue and if not like they choose another one.

2) A top notch automobile company chooses the best cricketer of the year for their endorsement. The player has performed phenomenally great last year and this automobile has several features that exceed customer's expectation. So for informal endorsement of brand, he is the right brand ambassador.

3) Advertising People were in search of two comic characters for a beverage advertises. Recently there was a comedy show in which 4-5 characters played phenomenal play. They have seen this show and approached two actors. They signed the contract and represented the brand.

4) Mr. Clean is working with a MNC for last 20 years. Over the years he has achieved a descent name with the help of their hard work, patience, talent, risk taking ability, calm nature and excellent personality which keep customer delighted. Organization nominated them to represent the organization in international innovation conference to be held in international

destination. 200 companies will be part of this event and Mr. Clean will present the new products presentation.

5) Hitesh is a skilled welder. He has finest skill of TIG welding. He has welded thinnest joint with radiography quality joint many times. There was exhibition of international welder's conference and company has nominated him to represent for company in this conference. In conference everyone was so impressed with his skill and expertise and many of them suggested him to prepare on line videos of his skill so that many of us can accept it as ideal and work to improve their skill also. Company thought on this proposal and with due delegation decided to go for it. They appointed professional video shoot services and recorded skill of 10 best welderslike Mr. .Hitesh and shared on their website as well as other social platforms to showcase skill of their welders and hence quality of their product.

Friends these are some of the example of brand ambassadorship. Initially you are known for employee of particular organization. Over the years you practice the work habits, work culture, typical mannerism, specific communication and general social behavior which create your personality. After some years you earn your name and become a true brand ambassador of your own name!

People co-relate product with their brand ambassadors. It is general belief that when such a reputed person endorsing something means he must have seen the ingenuity of these products else his own reputation may be at stake. Same thing happens with employees of any organization. During interview, Human resource and line managers take due care to fit candidates personality, achievements, track record and experience should match with organizations brand image in market, recent performance and business challenges ahead. Can this person transform the organization quickly? Can he influence his team and associates? Can he make peace with every conflict and drive organization through crisis in future? All these points are taken into consideration when you are interviewed for specific leadership roles.

Brand ambassadors are especially skilled and highly committed individuals. People generally follow them and try to implement improvement suggested by them or steps taken by them during their career journey. Struggle of these super achievers act as benchmark for million aspirant which make them a great idol. Hence brand ambassadors take due care to be socially admirable, descent and encouraging all time. This makes their followers inspired and confident.

The skill of brand ambassador is all about discipline, efforts and brand image. Practice this skill with right value inclusion in our personality.

Hope you liked this! Let's take a pause!

SKILL 33: EXPLANATION SKILL

PHOTO CREDIT : MEDIEN STURMER, UNSPLASH.COM

Good Evening Friends,

Welcome to new chapter of Explanation skill!

> *"Explanation skill is the ability to tell facts, experience and inclination about a subject matter to persuade, convince and create trust! It resolves doubts and makes things easy to understand which perhaps difficult. The end result of successful explanation is public acceptance!"*

The best examples of explanations:

1) Mr. & Mrs. Cool are looking for their new house in a prestigious housing project announced few days back. They reviewed the scheme , understood the plan , seen the RERA registration details , understood discount of stamp duty , seen distances of nearest landmarks and daily necessities like school, college , hospital , shopping mall . With this complete review, they decided to visit site location on one of the Sunday. On visit, they welcomed by the courteous project staff and graciously requested them to suggest which kind of flat they want to book. He given total necessary information same in line with advertisement and also told those to show sample flat which is neatly decorated and furnished. They gone for site visit and impressed with the accessories, floor space, design of interiors and rooms, city view from different floors in an animated video, list of amenities and parking area. He explained all the details of the project in such fluent and easy English that this couple was almost convinced about the status and prestige associated with this project. The staff also shown the pre-booking list and also shared socializing platform this project offers to lead a stress free, happy and comfortable life in natural environment in city's hustle. The explanations tuned in his favors and Mr. & Mrs. Cool booked fourth Floor River facing flat after

two day! The price of this 2BHK flat was 70 Lakhs!

2) Mr. Technique was presenting in an international trade presentation. He was associated with brand for more than five years and working as area sales manager. His personality was jolly and dynamic. He used to convince people with very very easy and likable style of expressions. When people used to talk with him, it was all laugh, contentment and happiness. The charm he used to create during interaction was absolutely real because not a single time he presents incorrect information. He used to be with the product all time, hence he was complete expert of products lifecycle details. In this event few delegates asked him few rough and tough questions , but with his unique ability to resolve questions into tactful easy answers he convinced delegates and received instant order book of the product in exhibition . The cost of product was 25 Lakhs!

3) A highly disappointed team of workmen approached Mr. Hope regarding technical issues they are facing with new product design. They were insisting their designer should visit the shop to explain them how things can be worked out so easily. New design was taking hell lot of time and because of which they are not able to contribute for productivity as per earlier track record which may affect business profitability. They were insisting for easy preparation of jigs& fixtures to make their work easy, fast and of right

quality. Mr. Hope quietly listened to their queries. He referred to drawing and released quality plan. He reviewed the job file in which jig and fixture drawing was referred. However the required dimension was incorrectly spelt which was creating difference in accuracy of fixture by which prototype approval was under hold till document correction. He explained this issue clearly and suggested to carry out other two activities which can be done by the time this issue get resolved as team is working on it. Other two steps can be done now and in final assembly, we can check everything, so there will not be any miss out or difficulty. But what about production? The answer was, the production will continue as it is, no worry, this is one of the path braking product of our total offerings. It is expected that sale will boost 60% once this product hit market. So put your complete dedication to make this product is grand success. Team got inspired and suggested number of suggestions and feedback and worked seamlessly to deliver the result. Sales boosted by 58% and everybody were so happy of their achievement. Mr. Hope got promotion as manager and a wonderful salary hike! Double!

Friends, hope you liked this chapter. Try hard for your skills; this is the only proven way of success.

Let's take a pause here!

SKILL 34: DEMONSTRATION SKILL

PHOTO CREDIT : MUSEUAMS VICTORIA, UNSPLASH.COM

Good morning friends,

Hope you are doing fine! Welcome to this chapter of demonstration skill.

> *"Engineering is all about applying principles of nature to create useful product & services. The inventors have to demonstrate his achievement to share knowledge with people by which they can use this invention for their related usage. "*

Through knowledge of functionality is core requirement to possess demonstration skill. Its perfect example of hand & eye co-ordination. The person demonstrating his typical skill has mastered that skill over years of practice and only after that he can confidently present with people.

The smoothness with which this skill is shown reflects the perfection level of skill. How many time we see in athletics the variety of aerobics stunts. We are stunned by seeing their flexibility, speed, accuracy and more of all their courage to perform the most dangerous physical actions. An error of few second also can cause serious injuries to its performer. So a thousand time structured training and practice is required before presenting this skill with public.

Generally we give basic idea about the invention or new product to people. We explain the need behind developing this product. Most of the time such need is related to regular life's challenges. And solution provided is claimed to surpass that challenge. This creates a very good understanding about the product. In next step, the basic structure, various opening and connections and their functionality is explained along with typical machine setting. When product start working and we see result of what is told versus what is seen, we start believing in product almost instantly.

The product is demonstrated at all possible service conditions. We get feel of wide scale usage of the product in variety of challenging situations for which product is designed. With achievement of satisfactory result the demonstration get completed. After which instructor may call few people from available viewers to participate in the demonstration and try from their side also. People test this product and find suitable for their purpose and then purchase it!

When a new product is purchased, customer is not aware about its complete functionality and there are chances that because of miss handling of product, there can be issues with its performance. Also the product can be used by so many users at same location. Hence a one time demonstration to everybody is very very essential. When people test the product in front of instructor two things happen, first is instructor note the first time feel of customer with their product offering as people give response and reaction to product features. This response helps to develop further stages of product according to requirement. Second thing, instructor observes the ease of actual handling of people and to facilitate its smooth use, they try to develop more and more simpler design. This way of democratizing the product makes product popular and it help to boost its sales!

When demonstration is being given, assistant to instructor may receive all feedbacks in details and later the complete development team work on it to improve product features to boost its sale and scale of production. This way demonstration helps to generate instant user friendliness of product which creates trust.

Is there any difference in training and demonstration? Yes, demonstration is part of training with the difference that in training you receive certain course material; there are practicals and exam at the end of training to certify from a recognized body of certification. With such certification, you may certify others on attaining certain levels of proficiency. In demonstration, the basic idea is about use of product, here no exam or no certificate. At the most, one can get approval when demonstration is given and can express their comfort of usage of product. Demonstration is customer –supply concern while training is teacher – student concept! Here lies the difference!

Along with main product, it is suggested to carry all accessories of product. With this customer get feel of several add ins and multiple usage of product and also understand the versatility of the product. What happens when demonstration fails because of technical issue in product? Here the skill of instructor works. Instructor is trained about kind of issues can actually arise during demonstration. They may open the product in front of people and note the defect and repair or rectify it with available tools and tackles. This instant action also creates trust. But for a new tested product, such chances are rarest!

Friends, hope you liked! Every skill needs practice and determination. Practice this skill with proper handling of product. Demonstration means effortless handling of the product! Let's pause here! ✍

SKILL 35: LOGIC APPLICATION SKILL

PHOTO CREDIT : JAPHETH MAST , UNSPLASH.COM

Dear Friends,

Good Morning & Welcome to this chapter of skill of logic application. Let's surf this!

> *"Logic is application of all possible conditions to arrive at exact conclusion. There is certainty with occurrence of effect because of its cause. The mathematical relation with cause and relations makes logic work flawlessly!"*

Logical Application Example 1:

"Happy" joined a car training center and after few days of training actually drive the vehicle. During first drive, he encountered common hands –eye co-ordination issues but on third and fourth practice he drives smoothly. He understood and used all road signs properly and got his learning license. After few days, he got his permanent license also. On a first long travel through Ghats section, he really feel the tricks of driving, speed changes and attentions required to drive the vehicle smoothly. This helped him to understand the real reasons behind strict traffic rules and their relation with our own lives. He sensed there is logic in drafting these rules, why somebody will force somebody to drive vehicles at suggested speed limit; it is because if these limits are crossed, there are chances of loss of control and in traffic chances of fatalities. This convinced him to follow all traffic rules not only in Ghats but also in normal city roads.

Logical Application Example 2:

"Ganesh "written software to generate result of a mechanical testing. The traditional way of mechanical testing is coupled with a transducer converting mechanical movement into equivalent electric signal which was fed to logic gate arrangement of AND, OR, Ex-OR , IF-THEN , this system used to create digital input and which was displayed on monitor in both printable and sharable form . While building logic for this software, he studied all normal test steps, studied literature and finalized relation between standard test sample and its result at various loading condition. Based on this relation he created full scale scenarios of mathematical values and their equated results. This prepared necessary database for result display. When he coded this relationship with value attributes, he find, it is showing correct values in test. The use of empirical relationship which was established in technical literature helped him to understand the logic of successfully running this software. On a trail day, he actually witnessed the testing and observed machine is exactly displaying result which was shown on analogue display unit. This way he digitalized the logic of machine which helped to carry out and record the test result automatic way on a click of start button. This increased speed of operations and improved efficiency with capacity to handle urgencies. What was the logic behind this digitalization? Ganesh knew mechanical system will not create electric signal on its own and software or PC will not sense mechanical properties on its own. We need a connector which can convert mechanical signal into electric signal, so he introduced a transducer. He studied type of transducers and selected best match. This triggered software and made total package works well on constant basis.

Logical Application Example 3:

Mr. Joy is a businessman and they are running a clothing business. They like to innovate their product and they offer it at great price which is very very affordable to major class of their customers.

Everyone is curious to know the key of this good quality-less price success logic, when asked in a success interview magazine, Mr. Joy share their success story. The design of their product is done with careful study of recent fashion trends across the globe. As fashion is time bound, they have to critically find out near equal forecast of their demand according to social conditions and festive seasons. They start manufacturing of their product just there month before festivals with huge pool of skilled craftsman working with them. This team suggests wonderful ideas and gets their in-house appreciation. This culture of innovation makes sure that every design is great and appeals their client. Secondly because of marketing on firm's website and e-commerce platform, their product is well known and with professional tie up with logistics, it reaches within time to customer. This help to boost sales. Mr. Joy build logic of selling their product through e-commerce website and internally they have developed the culture of innovation and eco-system of skilled craftsman and efficient logistics tie up to deliver what is intended at reasonably less price by taking advantage of economy of scale. This is the simple logical success funda!

Friends, logic resolves problems and make things easy to understand and work upon. Think from all possible outcomes of certain event and choose the right way! This is what application of logic mainly!

Hope you liked this chapter! Let's pause here! ✍

SKILL 36: INITIATIVE SKILL

PHOTO CREDIT : MARTEN BJORK, UNSPLASH.COM

Good Morning Friends,

Welcome to yet another chapter – Initiative skill!

> *"All good things have one thing in common. They start on time, they end on time. This is possible because planned initiatives are properly implemented. Initiative is initial energy & internal drive which attracts you to start and go for the challenges!"*

Let's see this imaginary story:

It is annual national technical presentation contest organized by Caliber Engineering College! Mr. Siddha is event organizer and this was their initiative to organize such event to promote knowledge sharing within national engineering talent along with guest lecture series of five days.

Mr. Siddha formed an executive team of ten students and 3 assistant professors. They created a beautiful presentation about event idea and major details and uploaded on college website and professional networking platform. They also given sponsored advertise in newspapers and communicated event details on national engineering college forum which host all aided and non-aided engineering colleges.

The schedule of five days was divided into two parts. First part deals with guest lecture of two hours while second part included national level paper presentation of ten shortlisted papers. The last 2 hours of last day of event were reserved for prizes and result declaration along with high tea and group photo event! There were 2 short breaks and one lunch break and total day span up to 8 hours, 10 AM to 6 PM.

They give advertise two month before and invited paper for panel review. Panel was formed with alumni of college working with corporates, scientific institutes and entrepreneurs. There was no entry fee for the event and the whole event was sponsored by big auto giant of the city. Mr. Siddha has fond association with this organization and major of their research work is widely accepted and implemented in their organization by way of a professional technology & research tie up! Prizes of event are sponsored by other three organizations where college alumni hold prestigious positions.

To their response, they received 200 papers from different part of the country in which they shortlisted 55 papers and send individual invitations to their presenters. The remaining 145 papers were planned to display on event website post event as knowledge sharing purpose.

The stay and meal arrangement of 55 students along with their 1 companion was done by college in nearby three star hotels, the bill of which was completely free as this owner expressively told college administration to provide him chance of noble service in helping for this event.

The travel tickets were subsidized up to 100% and city's leading travel company was co-sponsor of this event. This company also deals with daily commute of students of college.

So ,in all this initiative was completely meant for absolutely free technical festivals and talented 55 papers got chance to present here with bonanza of price money up to 3 Lakhs for first rank, 2 lakhs for second and 1 lakh for third rank and 10,000 for balance 52 papers and certificate for remaining entries.

The event happened as per the planned schedule with inauguration from eminent personality in scientific field from city along with their foreign delegates. Guest lecture series started with guidance about new normal and role of engineers in today's tech driven world. Which is followed by paper presentation by student? This schedule continued for five days and on last days winners are declared with their paper subject specialty in the mind of judges.

Felicitation, high tea and informal networking happened in last two hours and few principles also shared their feedback about event via video conference and physical presence. The whole event was a major success for Mr. Siddha and he congratulated whole team of 3 assistant professors, 10 students and complete staff along with all participant for their whole hearted contribution in this event.

It is this initiative and relation building skill that goes long way and created an all-inclusive, participative and encouraging event in a very very lively, funful and thoughtful environment. During these five days student learnt lots of organizing skills along with several paths breaking paper presentations about latest happenings in tech world. This helped to large volume of college channels subscribers! Hope you like this chapter!

Let's pause here!

SKILL 37: RELATIONSHIP MANAGEMENT SKILL

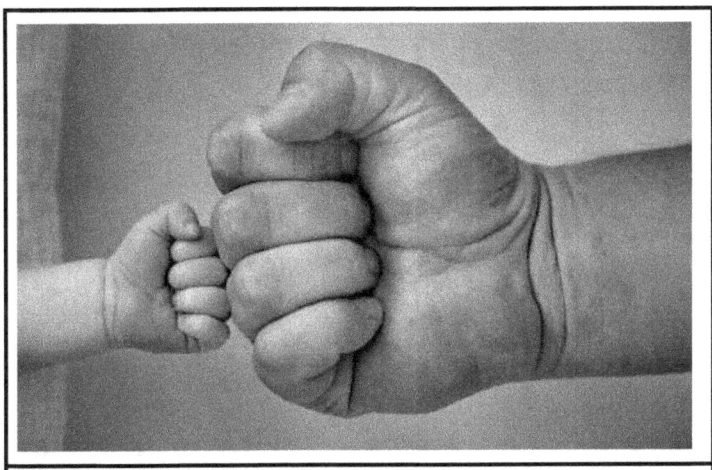

PHOTO CREDIT : NORBERT HENTGES, UNSPLASH.COM

Dear Friends,

Welcome to this chapter of relationship management skill.

> "Relations are meant for long term pleasant association of people, objects and surrounding. Relations foster with trust, care, support and understanding. Its two way street in which exchange of thoughts, actions and humor need to be an integral part! "

Perfect Relation Management imaginary story:

Abhyuday is seasoned material manager and he looks after procurement of special purpose parts. These parts are required for R& D jobs where constant innovation take place. Abhyuday has regular dealing with three suppliers who are expert in imported part purchase. These suppliers have long term presence in market and as Abhyuday is their regular client, they always give priority whenever he orders something.

Before reaching to a stage of such trust, an incidence was happened few months back. In supply of a particular ordered item, by mistake one supplier has provided a part of less capacity and rating than it is ordered. The part TC was correct but supplied parts serial no and its rating nameplate has got a technical issue. Hence this part was on hold at receipt end and hence supplier and material buyer called for resolution. Buyer has seen the issue along with supplier but supplier was showing reluctance in changing this part because nameplate was found in damaged condition during handling and because of which there was error in reading its details which caused incorrect part supply. This issue went to Abhyuday. Abhyuday called supplier and taken contact details of part manufacturer. He talked with concerned official and told them about real situation. He also sends photos of TC and damaged nameplate and suggested to file a DMAIC report to its supplier to avoid such careless handling. The original part supplier agreed to his systematic approach to resolve the issue in meaningful way and he agreed to supply the new part with upcoming consignment within three days and assured to store return his part so that he can carry out re testing and modify the nameplate with new record. Just provide him a weeks' time to approve this return procedure in their system. This sounds nice with everybody and this way Abhyuday managed & resolved the issue with supportive intervention with supplier, receipt QC and original part supplier.

Since then, there is good reputation of Abhyuday with all suppliers and whenever such conflicting situations occur, he has trained his reporting buyers to deal with situation with quality approach to keep things clear and transparent. That's the reason, his word is respected and priority is given for his work when he requests. In normal situations, his buyers do the tricks to ensure minimum conflicts reach at his end. This complete network of material planning is perfect example of relationship management.

Here it was not Abhyuday's part of work to intervene with supplier's supplier, but since he is well aware of international transactions and general business relation he helped his supplier to co-ordinate things for themselves. He could have used harsh word to supplier and may order to provide part at earliest else he will apply debit to his invoice but he has not done that. The reason was value of a person, his relation with organization and the current severity of part supply. He crosses checked with general manager, the ultimate dispatch date and taken concession of 2 more days post reporting this issue. General manager was fine with this and they suggested their shop planning person to amend production schedule accordingly. This has set the peace with every section and allowed supplier to fast track his activities of supply. Hope you liked this story.

Few Essentials of Good Relationship Management:

1) Respect time of each other.
2) Understand exact requirement and supply in full .In shortages or errors inform instantly.
3) Every problem has solution. Talk openly, genuinely and clearly.
4) Accept errors when they are, conflicting arguments wastes everyone's time.
5) Actions are best indicators of good relations. Take positive, timely action to move thingsfaster.
6) Maintain informal touch with people, it helps to meltdown hard rocks!
7) Both personal and formal e-mail communication is required. E-mails stand as your proof in case of more information enquiry. Crate specific folders.
8) Celebrate success and special achievements together. This increase trust and engagement.
9) In crisis, support each other and stay united. Problems get resolve with minor adjustments.
10) Connect more people with your network. Strength is best indicator of good relationship management skill. Hope you like it! Let's pause here! ✍

SKILL 38 : DEAL CRACKING SKILL

PHOTO CREDIT : CYTONN PHOTOGRAPHY, UNSPLASH.COM

Good Morning Friends,

Welcome to this new chapter of deal cracking skill.

> *"Deals are agreements of supply. One wins on cost, one wins on need. Fair deals take care of mutual benefit. "*

Friends, business is all about deals. You have to carry out various purchases and you have to supply your products and services to your customers on regular basis. In all such cases you have to interact, communicate and settle with many known and unknown people. Any first of a kind deal has certain protocol of dealing. When its business, you organize your meeting with prior appointment .Your sales co-coordinator visits customer site or customer visit your sales office to discuss about deal or you may meet at third party location convenient for business.

In the meeting you present your offering or services to potential customer. Customer listens to it, ask few queries and decide to purchase your product. Before purchasing, you discuss commercial details and negotiate to arrive at suitable price acceptable to both parties. This is the deal cracking.

Before meeting with you, the customer may have meet with several other competitors or he may have invited tenders from different supplier of same part. Out of shortlisted tenders, he must have selected you for meeting and after his satisfaction may have finalized an order with you.

On your side, you may have number of customer to serve for. They may be repeat customers, one or two time buyer or may be first time buyer. Accordingly you have to set the terms of your dealing with these customers. In repeat customer, there are standard requirement most of the time. Customer needs same part, product or service with change in quantity or same quantity as per his need of particular moment. Rates are already negotiated, only work balance is in case there are price changes because of market fluctuations, you have to update your price and tell it to customer. Such price hikes are within the affordability of customer and he pays you the premium price for your product quality and ease of service.

There are few customers who suggest your brand to their friends and relatives. In such cases, although these customers are first time buyers for you, you got recognition of your brand which is expressed by one of your customer which built initial trust level with you. With few queries and price knowledge, the new customer also purchase from you. As you supply your services and products, this goes on increasing and day by day because of your ability to communicate effectively, deals with courtesy and because of your product quality and availability you increase your customer base! This makes your business successful.

Some of the ways of a fair deal cracking:

1) Create beautiful product and easy services which fulfill the need of your customers.
2) Price your product with two selling principles, if you want instant sales with low profit margin, price with fewer profit margins. If you want to secure profit margin, price higher and wait till certain demand level and then increase your production to meet that demand.
3) Availability of sufficient stock is first and foremost thing for a descent business deals. When you have large volume requirement and supplier also has availability, deals happen easily with right price as you get your product and supplier get one time invoice for his ready stock which reduces his inventory and create space for producing more.

4) Once a business deal happens, prepare a well craft out schedule of supply of products or services or stages of its realization and set commercial terms accordingly. It means get advance on booking may be 10% of total deal, get 25% on first three stages out of ten total stages, 25% on next three stages, and 40 % before delivery to customer. When dealing with consumer products, set relation with stockiest and your distributors about best selling price and purchase price and sell accordingly.

5) Business is techno-commercial affair. Discuss technicalities of the deal in detail to make your commercial dealings easy. Charges are applied for remuneration to technical completion of product. So ensure you explain clear roadmap of your product realization with options of material, quantity and specifications. Specify variant of your offering.

6) Give time for business deals. Few deals happen very very quickly while few take months and years. Long term deals happen with certain fixed business policies and ethics of the trade.

7) Business credentials make business deals easy. Display your product or service with its all credentials. Which can be the best product of the year, recommended by certain agencies, or best among its product category? This gives preference of buying your product.

8) Do the deals with fairness of committed supply along with right quality and best price.

Friends, hope you liked this chapter.

Let's pause here!

SKILL 39 : SPORTS SKILL

PHOTO CREDIT : ALEXANDER REDL, UNSPLASH.COM

Dear Friends,

Good Morning and welcome to this new chapter –Sport skill. Let's play it joyfully!

> *"Sports are fun & learn kind of exercise! They built our physique and provide us stamina, strength and flexibility to accept victory or defeat equally becauseyou have to start again from zero each time to win."*

Friends, in a competitive world you have to strive hard to reach your goals, to achieve progress and to stay healthy. Being healthy is result of all good habits in which good food, good thoughts and good exercise are equally important. Sports activity provides these necessary aspects of personality to every sport lover.

You take example of cricket, one of the famous sports and loved by millions and trillions! This sport require stamina , running capacity , strength , wisdom, decision making skill , field protection and playfulness to ensure right team working , joy of winning and supporting each other in challenging times.

It is a well-known fact that when you run, you increase your stamina, builds your muscle strength and improves breathing. The inhalation of fresh ,light air in early morning sunrise give you lots of positivity and hopes to start your day with full of enthusiasm and energy .

It is natural that when you play or exercise, your appetite improves and boosts your food intake. Which gives you strength and you perform at altogether different level.

As far as individual indoor & outdoor games are concerned, athletics play important role in challenging your status quo. Be it long jump or high jump, be it gymnastics or relay, be it weight lifting or chess, you have to apply your mind, body and soul to win. The feeling of win is positive and it boosts confidence and spirit of individual. At the same time, when you lose, you feel down for some moment but again strive hard to improve on your mistakes and play again. The moment, at which your skill level surpasses your competition, you win.

Sometimes in sports like cricket, various unexpected moments happen, which create fun, surprise and attraction of sport? A well running partnership breaks with wicket of one of the batsman and then total collapse happen within 15 overs and within 80-90 runs , while sometimes we see two six , two four which are treat to watch . Sometimes chasing become so interesting that even one delivery is also become a moment of surprise while sometime overs and overs required to break a partnership in test cricket. As a viewer, you study various skills easily.

You learn initiative , right decision making, priority setting , risk taking , achieving milestones, surpassing challenges, thinking out of the box, making partnerships , deciding strategies to control the game result in your favor by using innovative approaches .

As you go on playing for number of years, it builds your confidence and determination. Every time you enhance your performance you enter into different levels of the game which are local, district, state, national and international. Becoming an international person is not easy task. It takes phenomenal efforts to reach and stay at such levels.

Business and sports has lots of similarity. You see various up-down in the business where you need a winner vision and action to stay firm, cool and decisive. You can't make decision in hurry in a way they create several later challenges. You have to think from all angles before making a business decision because there is risk of financial failure. Finance is the name of business game. When you have healthy balance sheet, you can fulfill all your aspirations and can provide employment to so many people.

Sometimes in sports you need to set up surprise field spacing to catch the competition to think about vacant places. When they can't see a gap in your field spacing, their chances of escape minimizes which give you advantage to control the competition and become winner. It's all psychological tricks. The effects of environment affect our minds decision making capacity and some errors happen which make competition win.

So, sports always give you this cool head and bright thought of winning in life. Be it return on investment or net run rate, we have to either set a big target or chase a big target; we have to make sure we keep scoreboard ticking by singles and doubles. We may get fours and sixes and can get maiden overs. We have to ensure that such stage will not happen in our business that we need to hit four and six on every ball. This loses fun of the game and it became a stressful affair. The fundamental aim of sport is to enjoy stress free and healthy life. Hope you liked this chapter. Let's pause here!

SKILL 40 : MORALE BOOSTER SKILL

PHOTO CREDIT : VICTOR FREITAS , UNSPLASH.COM

Dear Friends,

Good morning and welcome to this chapter – morale booster skill!

> *"Morale is constant state of high energy. Its superlative state of one's mind that can fight stronglywith any adversity, this state of mind help you to perform better and quick. Keep a professional moraleto emerge as winner out of any situation!"*

Historic incidences have revealed that wars and battles were win with highest morale of troops and their leader. The leader is an ultimate fighter and he removes all obstacles that come in his way to ensure all round acquisition of intended territory for which the war is fought for. War used to happen to keep integrity and sovereign status of the country. There were attacks from enemies and leaders have to fight war to send enemy back out of their territory. This is must have skill for every fighter as freedom is most sought after necessity for every individual and nobody like to get ruled by indecent people.

Whenever we hear slogans like "Har Har Mahadev "or "Jay Bhavani, Jay Shivaji" we feel charged up! A certain picture strikes our mind. We visualize a war footing where all horses and elephants are marching towards each other, soldiers are running with full force and fighting with each other, we also visualize various war strategies are formed with team of ministers and king and accordingly war instructions are given. Every team leader of troop motivates his team with energetic slogans and with his mere voice; people get charged and do whatever it takes to become victorious. Valor is nothing but readiness to give 100% for the country. Soldiers give their 100% for their country in every challenging situation.

Be it a war or personal and professional life, we fight various untold battles. In a civilized society we have to fight a fight of various approvals, we have to understand and study kind of rejections and setbacks,

We have to boost morale of our team to perform better and stay stronger, we have to ensure there is unison in team and everybody works with unique purpose to excel and serve the client and society in meaningful way.

As there are attacks in war, there are various sudden changes in business also. A competitor will bring an altogether appealing product that it will divert your customer base. Better software will come into market which will provide same service with very very low price and on huge scale which make buyers purchase things through this e-platform. A political decision will happen which makes organizations to march toward cost efficient locations. There are challenges and management has to take appropriate measures to counter these situations.

So a businessman or entrepreneur has always needed to stay with high spirit of positive thinking, quick action and timely status check to ensure he is taking every winning step. Any casual approach during any stage of implementation of his plan creates delay or chances of fumble.

Historical events has shown moments of betrayal, cheating, loss through mischief, to avoid such events the king and his team used to establish internal security systems comprising of various special skilled troop who used to communicate with king and his team in a different format of communication . A well informed king always takes right decision at right stage.

In business same things happens. There are people and people have desires. There are chances of misconduct and hence there is system of control through various audits, cross functional approvals and customer feedback analysis. With these control, management ensure high morale of people with good profitability.

Few simple steps to boost your morale:

- Believe in your potential. You can achieve things for which you are trying hard, true and consistent!
- Read good material and detox your mind with regular meditation.
- Exercise regularly and maintain a regular health habits. Healthy body rests healthy mind.
- Share examples of victorious achievement with your team. This creates feeling of trust and encouragement.
- Always stay hopeful in every situation. Miracles happen when we possess courage and stay firm on our beliefs.
- When somebody is feeling low, talk with them, make them happy, try to find out root cause of their issue. People respond when we talk generously and act wisely.
- Chant your favorite slogan, song or speech that will drive you to move ahead every time.
- Always remember the start and visualize satisfactory end of every activity. This mindset helps boost your morale.

Hope you like this chapter! Let's take a pause!

SKILL 41: LISTENING SKILL

PHOTO CREDIT : ERIC MOK, UNSPLASH.COM

Dear Friends,

Good afternoon! Welcome to this new chapter of Listening Skill!

> *"Listening is the ability to grasp knowledge, experience and variety of situations. When you listen carefully, you don't need to face challenges which speaker already faced and overcome. It's the best contributor of a perfect communication."*

Better listeners learn faster. Slow listeners work longer. When a speech or communication happens, it is the ability of person to understand the subject, know the relationship with different aspect of communication, develop their own way to remember the things and finally answer the question with precise words.

When you are travelling, there is continuous announcement on station about arrangement of bus or train. If there is change in timing or change in platform, you get notification through such announcements. What will happen, if you do not listen to these instructions? You may miss the bus or train or you have to wait for long hours.

When you are writing in exam, there is written instruction regarding which questions are mandatory? Suppose in one of the question paper , it is written , " solve any three out of five with question number 1 mandatory , here with inclusion of question no 1 into answer sheet , you are left with 4 questions from which either of two to be attempted. But if you skip question no 1 and solve other three questions, you will not get marks for other question. So clear cut listening and understanding is very very important.

In schools and colleges, we are constantly doing knowledge grasping activity. We do ask questions but our scope of work is limited. We are receptors of knowledge. When we are at work, we are applying this knowledge to create product or services. Here nobody teaches or talks like a teacher but we have to obey instructions given by our reporting authority to make sure we work correctly. With the passing years, we know our work and then afterwards it's a silent operation. Here whenever we do not listen to standard operating procedures, drawings, specifications, special instructions and statutory requirements, we have to face challenges such as error in product, customer complaint on quality, discomfort at customer end, and interrogation at various customer support forums, loss of production, loss of profit, and loss of customers.

When we listen to written or verbal instructions which are correct, we find it easy to complete our work. There is common understanding with whole team and we find it very very easy going out there.

Some of the common listening practices:

1. Start a conversation with confident handshake and pleasant smile.
2. Initiate the discussion with common reference.
3. Tell frankly what kind of information you need out of this discussion.
4. Make sure you provide factual notes to endorse your views.
5. When other person will start providing desired information, listen it carefully. Maintain positive eye contact and nod whenever you agree to the facts.
6. When he finishes, express your own views on matter and seek his response.

7. It may happen that other person may respond or not, but try to discuss the matter in detail.
8. With proper fine tuning, people open up with confidence and they share you details related to subject matter.
9. Question in between! Questions have answers. Either true or false. You can always verify and insist for its correctness in return dialogue. If answer is correct, you need not to call again, if answer is false and you verified with person who has told you, he will understand his mistake and provide correct information next time. This is all part of active listening, starting with trust and building trust by cross verifying given information with respect to actual facts.
10. Active listening has positive dialogues which create frank talk, moment of humor and interpersonal emotional touch which many time heals mental baggage's and make relation strong and affectionate.

Friends, every good listener become a best speaker after some time. Every best speaker becomes a good leader after some time. Every leader becomes a successful person after some time. Every successful person indirectly influences other person and creates the same way of listener, speaker, leader and successful person for others. This creates a society of successful people which is rich, satisfied and happy! What else is required in life? Hope you like this chapter. Let's pause here!

SKILL 42: INTERVIEW FACING SKILL

PHOTO CREDIT : CHRISTINA . UNSPLASH.COM

Dear Friends,

Good afternoon and welcome to this chapter– Interview Facing skills.

> *"An interview is a systematic approach to know personality of candidate to assess his or her fitness for role. A perfect match answers the questions with examples, data and detailed thought process to make their selection an easy task!"*

Life is journey of thousand miles with company of friends and family members. When we born and grows up we develop our senses with the help of surrounding environment and culture. We learn to walk, talk, listen, care and work with day by day's progress. Education is important of phase of life which exists till the end of life but predominantly first 25 years of life are meant for serious formal education to make us literate so as to face the real world when we become a responsible citizen.

During our upbringing, we come across several well-wishers, friends, philosophers and guide who shape up our personality by inspiring us, motivating us, by doing things for us, by providing material comfort for us. This exchange of development happens with various interactions at personal and group level. In such interactions we come across our general inclination, our interest and our decision making preference in response to a particular situation or problem. Because of this, the person accompanying us either appreciates our efforts or gives us improvement feedback to develop further. This all happens for our development.

On completing formal education when we decide to work as entrepreneur or as employee, we have to enter job world by passing examination known as interview. By the age of 22 years, we have acquired degree, good academic score but interaction with practical field person is altogether different exercise.

At various phases of your career you have to face different kind of interviews. Let us see these examples:

1) ***Interview of a Trainee Engineer :***

This interview is about your fundamental concept understanding, your general knowledge about company for which you are giving an interview, your academic record and your general interest and hobbies to understand you as a person along with any work shop related experience. The questions asked or aptitude test planned test your mathematical ability, your logical reasoning and analytical ability and your problem solving and decision making skill. You have to present your answers in neat, clean, easy way to make sure interviewer understood what you want to say. The proficiency of your communication act as your strength during such interview. Among the list of several candidates if your answers are found correct and if organization feels you are right candidate for position with your future career scope judgment, you get selected.

2) ***Interview For Supervisory Positions:***

These positions represent experienced candidates. This experience can be 2 year to 6 years. After first year of training and subsequent confirmation, you work in a particular department and start executing duties over there. Slowly you know your job and start achieving basic job knowledge, skill and proficiency. Interview of these positions means your contribution to field by way of improving efficiency of operations, by carrying our manpower development, by designing newer technological solutions, by carrying out research in allocated field. Your performance indicators, your promotion record and your credentials decide your path of success. These interviews are about tackling process challenges of day to day career.

3) ***Interview for Middle Management :***

Middle management positions act as backbone of the organization. These professionals are having experience of 10- 20 years of service. These interviews deals with your supervisory skill, your project performance and their timely execution, your cost saving and innovation inclination and more about your skill of dealing with people, problems and time with system approach.

4) ***Interview for Senior Management Profiles:***

These are some of the most anticipated positions of one's career and deals with knowing your personal influence, team building capability, market thoroughness, strategy development and result oriented initiatives. These are positions of extraordinary human potential! Hope you liked these concepts! Let's pause here!

SKILL 43 : CONTINGENCY MANAGEMENT SKILL

PHOTO CREDIT : BERNARD HERMANT, UNSPLASH.COM

Dear Friends,

Good afternoon and welcome to the chapter of contingency management! Let's know some tough stuff!

> " Situations come to test our planning capability. Provisioning for contingency is best way to deal with unexpected challenges . It provide last hours comfort in crunch situation !"

Let's go through these short imaginary passages:

Case 1: Contingency for Urgent Fund:

In year 2019, firm WINNERS LTD recorded 10 % growth in their annual profit. It was the result of some wide scale digitalization activities which help to boost sales. 5 % profit is invested to further expand the digitalization process with addition of ten more customer relationship management kiosk at ten new cities. 5 % profit is saved for contingency fund account started from last two years.

Now because of sudden slowdown they restricted their expansion plan by 50 % and decided to implement it in two phases as things reach to normalcy. This strategy change was very much necessary in response to strict limitations posed by the situation.

Now because of reduced mobility they increased their digital operations by which they can fulfill the customer demand. This works well and helped them to perform 65% of their normal operational speed which was helpful to deal with this contingent situation.

They talked with their customers and supplier with step to step payment of funds which will not put additional pressure on working capital and business momentum does not affect to larger extent.

The provision made in contingent fund of last three year used to procure some urgent material to supply the in demand product of that situation and book moderate profits. This strategy in fact helped to boost digital expansion and make their growth story continue irrespective of challenging situations of business stability.

From that year onward, the management decided to double the amount in contingency fund to ensure seamless operations.

Case 2: Contingency Arrangement for Personal Education:

Dheeraj was a sincere student and he was thinking to do his MS from foreign universities. The educational budget was about few lakhs and that much money was not available with him. He decided to go for scholarship and applied for few institutes. The qualified amount was up to 60% and balance 40 % he has to manage on his own.

Dheeraj decided to wait for two year for his plan. In these two years, he did a job and start saving for his education. According to his estimates, he could save up to 10 % with his salary and for balance 30 % he has to look for another income source.

He decided to develop mobile applications. Coding was his favorite skill and by using this skill he has prepared two science applications which will become helpful for student to refer all scientific formulas used in Engineering streams. This exercise was strenuous and he referred to 5 engineering branches to collect data and compile in application. When he loaded the app, he got very very good response by which, to his surprise he managed the balance fund of 30%. With this success, he focused his effort to develop one more app and got similar success. This trick worked for him and he decided to keep this skill updated during his MS studies to become financially independent.

After few days, he completed his two years job contract and managed to go for his MS studies. Now he has enough fund to cut short the scholarship amount to 40 % and manage 60% funds from his job saving and income from mobile application development. Now as the app download increases, the income increases, with this logic he decided to repay scholarship amount systematically to ensure some needy student get this benefit. So arrangement of passive income source through app development act as contingency arrangement for Dheeraj which made his education possible as per his plan and specific job experience to know real world. Friends, if you want to do it, then there are many ways. Just stay calm, use your head and become achiever!

Hope you liked this story and also the skill to manage contingency. When you tie ourselves to limited skills we become stagnant as time flies, but when we keep ourselves updated, we improve ourselves beyond our expectations! Let's pause here!

SKILL 44 : ADVERSITY & SURVIVAL SKILL

PHOTO CREDIT : DAVID GAVI, UNSPLASH.COM

Dear Friends,

Good Evening & welcome to this new chapter of Adversity and survival skill.

> " *Survival is result of constant endeavor of excellence ! Adversities come and with thoughtful efforts they are surpassed . The way we put our effort decides our longterm existence in any system & its surrounding!*"

We don't have control on so many things! We can't sense so much happening. We can't predict our future exactly. Some situations come to test our fullest potential. Such situations are known as adversities. Survival in such situations need some extra efforts, some pre planned provisions and indomitable spirit of human capital.

Response to adversities is a skill. Let's see following steps to deal with adversities and survive through this situation:

Adversity Survival Skill:

1) Adversities can be related with finances, people or time. Learn the type of adversity to devise their response well ahead of their individual or united occurrence.

2) Dependency over single income source freezes limits of safety and make you vulnerable to adversities. So try to have at least one smallest income source which can take care of you and your family's two time meal in case of adversities. Never use income from this source for regular life expenses which can be managed from your best income source. Keep it in safe investment installment so as they remain safe as well as grow with time.

3) When it is necessary spend up to certain extent, save some money although you wish to spend a lot! This good time saving will act as your support stick in adversities.

4) Installments, Medical expenses, lifestyle budget all are important aspect of financial literacy. Decide a certain level of expenditure according to current level of income.

5) In adverse situation always stay calm and confident. Analyze the situation for its root cause and point to point details of its occurrence to ensure you use same path or similar counter path for your escape.

6) When you have problem with availability of people for doing work, there are several arrangement by which people can be arranged to deal with adversities. Hire contract people, train your regular staff for additional skill – at least one multitasking skill to take care in urgent situations, there are third party service providers for most of the professional services- with descent premium cost you can manage completion of task , maintain a certain surplus with very very critical work requirement . This way people management issue during their absence or delay can be managed.

7) When there is adverse time, think with fast speed about all possible actions that can be taken and instruct your complete staff to work on major causes. It strength of team which makes wonders of achievement in adversities related to time. Stay firm on your beliefs. Maintain best possible discipline in your team and surpass that challenging time. At the end you win and survive.

Friends efforts put in wrong direction always drive you to adversities, difficulties and nightmares! Always keep track your progress as you feel it necessary and right. Improvise on errors to plug them at right time. With passing time, seriousness of error increases because of which many new problems arrive, so finish pending errors or mistakes in right time before close of the day. Start new day with fresh hope in times of adversity. Every day brings different energy, keep trying and keep improving day by day!

There are typical people whose performance shines in adversities. This is surprising but it happens in reality with some special people. These people have faced several adversities in their life and hence they get clear understanding about response to such situations. Cherish such people as they act as torch bearers in difficult times.

In typical business world adversities are common as no one gets free meal. Everybody has to work hard, learn continuously and achieve their dreams with constant efforts. Only difference is, in difficult time you have to forget number of hours you put into service with respect to quality and impact of your efforts. It changes the result of the game you are facing!

Hope you like this chapter. Always believe in your true potential. When we determine to stay strong, our energy levels support us to overcome the barriers put up by situations. Let's pause here!

SKILL 45 : LOAN REPAYMENT SKILL

PHOTO CREDIT : RUPIXEN, UNSPLASH.COM

Good Evening Friends,

Welcome to chapter of loan repayment skill.

> " Loan is arrangement of instant fund on approval that make the path of your dream possible . When availed loan is totally repaid with interest , it gives confidence of perfect planning , constant earning and to raise capital for your dream business!"

Friends, when we are living in 21st century, the century which is better known as Computer edge and knowledge economy, every youth has seen rise in aspirations to develop their potential in achieving this new edge skill. With increased urbanization, several employment opportunities are available at major cities and global destinations. Because of which, people with low to medium income level are finding it difficult to meet their dream. However their dreams are possible to fulfill with availability of various purpose loans which are displayed by banks and other financial institutes,

Let us take example of various loans and their repayment trends:

1) **_Educational Loan :_**
   This loan is availed and provided for completing your dream education. The installment has to provide with comfortable repayment period. Based on your need you can decide maximum qualified loan amount and your repayment period. All you need to do is to complete your education with descent academic track record and be engaged in business or in an employment opportunity. Generally candidate save their initial salary may be 30-40 % to arrange for EMI and repay it with fastest tenure to account for less interest and more saving.

2) **_Home Loan :_**
   Once you get confirm in your service or you settle in your business, you start aspiring about a

descent home in reasonably good, quiet and happy society. When you search for nearby property, you observe distance and price has inverse relation. A home near to your office cost much higher than one which is bit outside. In one city, however, there is not big difference in price, so you go for your best choice and book a home with qualified amount of home loan. In some cases percentage of loan availability is depends on your in hand income with maximum threshold of loan amount. Balance amount you have to raise from other sources.

In a permanent employment up to 60 years of superannuation, you get various plan of tenure along with their rate of interest. You have to consider income tax benefit available on first property and accordingly work out a suitable loan repayment period in which you find your future income will be enough to take care of other life's priorities.

Generally, EMI goes through salary. With annual increments, with passing years this burden is relaxed and people repay this loan within ten to fifteen years or less safely with moderate financial discipline.

3) **_Car Loan :_**

With life's necessity and aspirations, your own four wheeler attracts you. This is generally period of your life with starting of family life. Observing the market trend, you shortlist your four wheeler brand and approach for loan availability. If money is available with you, then no issue but when things need lots of financial support, you have to take advantage of various load schemes. By the time you avail this loan, you have repaid your housing loan up to certain extent. Now with your safe calculations you have to adjust both EMI. Generally this loan is repaid in 3-4 years.

4) **_Business Loan :_**

After a descent stay in corporates, some people decide to start their own operations and startups to achieve their dreams and to provide employment opportunities to others. In some cases, they start with some own or borrowed initial seed capital. However there is various start up schemes which provide limited capital. When your business sets with your hard work, market presence and continuous customer, you repay your business loan and take new loan to expand your business. A stage reached where you become loan-free and operate on your own. All you need a descent, practical financial literacy and right skills to deliver your products and services.

Friends, there are various aspirations which can be fulfilled with descent loan scheme. Hope you liked it!

Let's take a pause here! ✍

SKILL 46 : MACHINE HANDLING SKILL

PHOTO CREDIT : GLENN HANSEN , UNSPLASH.COM

Good Morning Friends,

Welcome to a new chapter – Machine handling skill!

Let's check few points.

> "Machines are built with logic and mechanism. A machine has display and internal arrangement of functional parts. Understand internal working so as you can handle the machine comfortably!"

In an industrial and office environment there is presence of number of machines to get work done. In modern societies, to live comfortably, we use lots of special purpose machines. So a detailed understanding about safe use and careful handling of machines is very much necessary. In normal life we use Mobile, Vehicle, and Computer, Water Heater, LPG stove, Printers, Laptops and many more machines based on individual lifestyles.

In industrial environment, we are qualified and trained to use various machines which can be either production machine, testing machine or maintenance machine. A production machine will help you to produce large volume of products. There will be particular capacity of these machines based on its size and rating. One can easily understand about output created by a particular machine. Based on this output and available demand one can choose requirement of machine. Now handling of these costlier machines is important task and there is direct linking of incorrect handling and loss of production. So all machine operators are given systematic training about uses of machine, its internal structure , its display unit, its electrical connection , it set up and available methods for which this machine can be used and cannot be used, daily cleaning and oiling requirement , how to keep it after use . Based on these notes, a systematic training programme is arranged by which individual performance is assessed and task is allocated to best performer. With practice and efforts, he becomes a skilled machine operator. A skilled machine operator exactly knows about machine parameters and their setting. He knows with which machine settings we can get quality output. If its welding machine , welder or welding operator exactly know which welding document to be referred for selection of current and voltage for arc welding, how much gas pressure to be kept, what kind of inertness is required to keep weld pool away from contamination, how the material behaves during various stages of welding! By noting and practicing these technicalities on a test piece, he adjusts all parameters suitable to his skill of welding and completes the respective weld. When this weld is tested for its strength properties, if the parameters are used correctly there is complete fusion and solidification of weld joint with achievement of weld properties more than parent metal which was joined together.

In testing machines, we have to understand the principle and international specification governing the testing along with a true and sincere mind. Testing is a very very big ethical duty and you have to remain firm with result you seen. If material meets test results, it's okay. In case the product doesn't meet the required properties, you have to reject it and try out retesting on another sample of same batch. If this sample passes the criteria, then another random samples are to be seen and tested, if this sample passes the criteria then you have to pass the test. A detailed analysis of failed test sample is need to done based on its type of fracture during test based on its macro and micro level studies.

With respect to international specification, there are requirements about no of test samples, their location, their identification, there loading on testing machine, setting of test environment, test hours and witness record and then actual result and its reporting as per recommended formal format with seal and signature of test house. Such machines include universal testing machine, hardness testing machine, Digital microscope, Spectrometer, PMI testing machine, Radiography testing unit, ultrasonic testing machine and loads of other machines.

Handling of maintenance related machine is basically about handling of tools and tackles. You need to understand required size of the tools like spanners, drills, screw drivers, pliers, various sensors and meters which display functional properties like potentiometer, electric tester. Here you have to open the machine and see current status of internal parts. There is relation between type of defect and its root cause. Maintenance engineer and mechanics are well aware of this knowledge. When we report issue, they check this system and look for any further damage. Once defect is noted, they replace, repair of rework to required standard and test for its functioning. On satisfactory result they handover to customer with necessary handling input suggestion for correct handling.

Friends, we hope you liked this chapter. Let's pause here!

SKILL 47 : TRUST BUILDING SKILL

PHOTO CREDIT : BRETT JORDAN , UNSPLASH.COM

Dear Friends,

Welcome to this chapter of trust building skill. Let's see how this skill is acquired.

> " Trust is the best example of successful human interaction . When you trust fully, you are relaxed about result of outcome because you are confident that be it true or false, it will be reported for sure! Such results can be dealt aptly later on !"

It takes year to build trust and second to break it! Why so much risk associated with breach of trust. Answer is simple. Loss of engaged party which believed in you and allowed you to associate with them. But is the breach of trust one sided affair. No! As per action of law of action and reaction, there is always equal and opposite reaction to every action. Hence there is 'n' no of reason before a breach of trust happens. So in a civilized society, it becomes necessary to build trustworthy relations!

In a technological world, trust is built in the system with the help of accurate true logic. True logic deals with options of possible human interaction with the machine serving a typical purpose and scope of its operation. Before usage, the manufacturer ascertains the users about use and applications of machine, its functioning and its safe handling guidelines. This is first step from manufacturer in creation of trust levels. He is transparent with his manufacturers test certificate .He has provided written manual for machine uses. He has provided trial work sample prepared by use of this machine at respective parameters to validate his claim. Now its operator's skill & responsibility to handle this machine carefully to receive desired outcome. It is his chance to take trust building step from his side. The way he handle the machine, he will get response. In many machine, the SMART LOGIC is built which make you aware about wrong handling of machine and hint you a system notification about wrong or unauthorized handling. This is done by taking authorization credentials at the start of machine to record who is using the machine in case problem is noted. Such systems also ensure to seek your permissions before going ahead. If you still want to go ahead, machine does its job and stop functioning. This logic of auto cut off is built in the system with the help of different sensors. If it is electric part used for limited heating purpose, there will be arrangement of a sensor unit which can measure the change in system temperature once it crosses set threshold level and cut off the current path automatically with the help of relay switch to stop increasing temperature. Once temperature goes below set minimum threshold it will again sense this temperature and operate in reverse fashion to activate relay to rise the temperature. In this way, this sensor system built trust with its user by providing required heating within range of temperature.

This is why Engineering systems speak for themselves through their performance. But what about its durability. Its fine that you have prepared a machine with smart logic , sell it but if it not durable , how can customer ensure he will use this machine for certain number of minimum years as he is investing huge money and he do expect return from his investments. The answer to this question is standardization. When a machine is built with durability concern, quality plays important role! In standardized method of manufacturing, you use specified tested material for particular application, you prepare product with best possible manufacturing practice and you package it with safe and secure handling options. This ensures your machine last long. There are many examples in which people tell, I have used this machine for years, but still its shine is permanent. Off course I clean it daily but the steel used for this machine really possess a very very good quality. This feeling sets sense of trust and attachment with your product or service offering.

In case of failure of product within warranty period, immediate replacement with basic evidences of mishandling is great step to build trust with your brand. When it is warranty period and your part fails, it has only two possibilities, either you have made a physical damage or the part is defective itself. So authorized service centers, with the help of standard checklist ask customer about their product handling and ensure right conclusion. When it is okay with product handling, they own the fault and provide either free of cost service of total replacement and necessary disposal of part in their reverse engineering system.

Knowledge is key element in building trust. When you have right knowledge , the person dealing with you assess and check with few questions, once he note your knowledge level , either he deals with you honestly or dishonestly . An honest person express his opinions frankly which are observed with its visible silent proofs and this builds trust. With regular interaction this trust grows. It is that much simple. Friend trust is base of every relation. Hope you liked this! Let's pause here!

SKILL 48 : NETWORKING SKILL

PHOTO CREDIT : ADEM AY , UNSPLASH.COM

Dear Friends,

Good morning and welcome to this new chapter- Networking skill!

> *"Networking is the ability to connect with people with building trustworthy relations irrespective of boundaries of cast, religion , education , income levels & status. Its human connection preserving humanity!"*

In old village days, what was so special about lovely living irrespective of very few material comfort resources. It's the wonderful company of nature and very very strong people relation and emotional attachment with each other. It was the networking with nearby friends , family members , villagers and various officials serving for village which make community a happy , neat , clean place .

Whereas in a city , there is huge community of people coming from different parts of nation to explore their interest , field of study and setting their career aspirations which may not be fulfilled in villages at that particular time frame. Here people are not living with each other from beginning but they maintain trustworthy relations with practicing healthy cultural habits of mutual respect, co-operation , work ethics and frankness of enjoying life to its fullest potential. Here everyone is clear about the contribution from their side to live in a society of like-minded individuals.

In a Global workplace, the trust level is simply built with the power of communication. Here your countries are different, your cultures are different, your work styles may be different but you are together to provide a product that fulfills your need at competitive price. This business association fostered by mutually agreeable terms and conditions of material supply and payment facilitation at product realization stages. This is coupled with respective international tax and duties . Which is again the techno political decision between the nations at large !

So in present situations , interpersonal communication and networking is become so much necessary to express your requirement and deal clearly and in a timely manner. There are various social networking platforms which are created by innovative creators to connect with each other easily , effectively and regularly with back up of what we have talked and decided to do .

Let's see some networking basics:

- Believe in your relation with which you wish to network . Network can be professional as well as personal . People live in group and groups have common interest predominantly.
- Sending and accepting connection request is a formal norm set by networking platform for virtual networking to respect the freedom of association of their users . Ensure you know the person at least in one physical meeting .
- Profile information and credentials speak for person's genuineness. Along with their employment details , career trajectory and testimonials shared by their friends and associates.
- What happen if you network with wrong person ! Nothing! All controls of decision are with you. You can always check the things with relevant formal or informal interrogation and trust building skill. I am providing this because you have

provided this stand act as expressing virtual genuineness.
- There are unwritten rules and understanding of common sharing. The whole idea of networking is make users aware about opportunities, right talent and pleasant association to co-operate each other.
- Professional networking grows with references, various national –international event and friendly social association.
- Personal networking grows with neighborhood, Participation in social & cultural events and help provided in crisis situation.
- Touch is common practice to cherish relations. When you connecting with each other, it is necessary to understand you speak with each other on formal or informal events. This helps in growing your interaction and trust with each other.
- In case of concern, miss understanding or issues , a personal face to face meeting resolves the matter.
- With years and constant communication, you know each other and it sets your credibility, identity and reputation. This helps in expanding your network in the form of friends, association to followers.
- People grow, excel and compete with correct networking. Humanity is key!

Hope you like this chapter. Let's pause here! ✍

SKILL 49 : NO FEAR ATTITUDE DEVELOPMENT SKILL

PHOTO CREDIT : URIEL SOBERANES, UNSPLASH.COM

Good Morning Friends,

Welcome to this chapter – No fear attitude development skill. Let's go fearlessly.

> " Fear is nearest hurdle to one's success . When we crossover fear , we get confidence and we put our efforts in such a way that we emerge as a winner!"

Since childhood, we have some kind of fears. We fear to climb, we fear to go alone outside our village or nation, we fear to look downwards from a tall building, we fear to write in exam, we fear to sing in front of people, we fear to start our business, we fear to swim in river or sea, we fear to learn driving, we fear to handle high voltage electric equipment's!

Why this fear factor comes in our way! The reason is worry of falling, worry of getting lost ,worry of falling down, worry of what people will say, worry of failure in business ,worry of drowning, worry of falling down , worry of electric shock , worry of our life , worry of losses , insecurity about future !

Once you find out these root causes, it gives clear idea of your mental and physical barrier. You decide to take action on this fear factor and build your physical strength by various types of exercise and things required to upgrade your knowledge of unknown, at the same time it is necessary to build your mental strength which is achieved by proper meditation, yoga and memory improving techniques. Beyond physical and mental strength improvement, there is another level of exceptional knowledge and experience of spiritual learning. This learning gives you a confidence of doing your deeds with great intentions, clear actions and without expectation of immediate outcome of your efforts. When you do the hard work with best dedication, commitment and all round thinking success in any endeavor is bound to come Development of this complete knowledge is known as becoming winner over your fears.

Curiosity and fear has a very very fond association. When you have fear, you are thinking about several losses but when you develop a thought process of facing these losses before they actually occur, you built a resistance system to tackle these losses and start taking counter measure to overcome your fears. So, when actual loss making event happen, you are well prepared to face this with its right measure. This trick helps you to avoid losses and ensure benefits.

Be it a student age, a professional age or a family man's mature age , when we are clear about cause and effect of any event , we get alert of that danger , prepare our plan of action , we do strong fight with that danger with our strength , when our strength surpasses the danger , we win ! That how the game of fear is won!

Fearless Attitude Checklist:

1) Ask yourself why I have this fear.
2) A self-talk always brings out all your fear on surface, hidden fears is difficult to manage, hence bring them of actionable surface. Share it with your dear ones or professional expert according to type of fear.
3) Friends, understand life in totality. Prayer has power of healing and providing mental strength .Practice prayers to become a strong willed

person. Will power defeats all fears hence be a strong carrier of your indomitable spirit.

4) When you have energy, let it be any fear, you face it. The force required to tackle these fears is provided by the energy received from your physical and mental strength.

5) The ability to think in far direction lead to understand consequences of certain fearful event. You prepare in advance and become successful.

6) Human mind is creator of fear and destroyer of fear. The body just support to perform this task by respecting to these decisions. Always think positive, in case of negative thoughts, practice spiritual remedies to believe in supreme power of almighty and sometime forget about your all fears.

7) Create several options in dealing with fear. When one option fails, other option brings you closer to success.

8) Try without fear of failure .Out of thousand unsuccessful efforts; it required one effort to record success. This is what fear science all about. Friends, hope you like this chapter. We have some of the ancient literature already available, try to read such books always. Enhance your knowledge, skill and experience level to emerge as a winner! Let's pause here!

SKILL 50 : UNWINDING SKILL

PHOTO CREDIT : SIMON MIGAJ , UNSPLASH.COM

Dear Friends,

Good Morning and welcome to this new chapter – Unwinding skill!

" We work , we work , we work & we unwind!"

Rest and relaxation is one of the important aspects of one's personal & professional life! In a life full of responsibilities, deliverables and commitments, we need "My time" to unwind and relax a bit to recharge again and perform better.

> *"In a fully packed market, you are working hard and suddenly your favorite song is played on cellphone by somebody, you moves up and keep work aside for 1 minute and enjoy the song. How it feels? Fresh & Recharged ! This is the power of unwinding!"*
>
> *" In a strict exam you are in the middle of the paper and you suddenly remembers a favorite joke shared by your friend , you feel happy andlaugh happily in your mind and start focusing more ! This is the timing ofunwinding!"*
>
> *" You are on a business tour for three days .After three days of meetings, discussion and decisions, you are fully exhausted and you need a break ! You have two days weekend waiting for you! Youvisit nearest tourist destination and forget yourself in this scenic atmosphere ! You feel young and fully energetic! This is the power of unwinding!"*

" You are relaxing on your holiday and an urgent phone calls come and you freeze your plans of that day and attend that urgency. Once that urgency is handled successfully, the whole team dealing with that situation feel happy and full of joy and you decide to spend that holiday evening in nearest snacks hotspot ! You chat, share jokes and relax ! This is power of bonding through unwinding!"

" You have carried out a research project by working day and night, you have met with several challenges, spend thousand hours on designing your innovative idea to realize its form, shape and size and you have produced a proto type of that product. You got successful trail and now planning to run the first batch of production. You created it and presented to market. After couple of days, enquiries start coming and sell of your product is started, within one month demand for your innovation is increased to 400% and you decided its full scale implementation by optimizing your production capacity and achieves up to 90% demand. On this achievement, you host a big party with your team and you celebrate your success to fullest ! This uplifts your spirit and inspiration to do more! This is power of unwinding ! Three hours of party and mouthful
energy, joy, satisfaction!"

Some Unwinding Tricks :

1) Hobbies, interest and sports are re creators of energy and enthusiasm, cherish & practice these things often to make everybody beautiful & successful.

2) Freshening up starts with morning exercise while unwinding starts with quiet free walk in the evening! This walk gives you satisfaction of the day and makes you feel relaxed and content! It also devise new plan to do some improvement next day in case you missed something. This is how successful people think and work mostly.

3) In every part of social and technical set up, need of intermediate break is planned to relieve unexpected stress which arise because of constant engagement of brain. In this break, brain rests and you feel relaxed. So always take short breaks after two –three hours of any kind of work.

4) We see in cricket, there is exchange of field placing after every over. This help to relax and try from other end. Its batsman's ability to stay on wicket while bowlers ability to take wicket from both end. The fractional moment of this unwind provide you to think different options and use the best one either to score a four for batsman or take a wicket for bowler! Always unwind for some time to increase stamina and quality of our work! Hope you liked this chapter! Let's pause here!

SKILL 51 : RELAXATION SKILL

PHOTO CREDIT : ALEX BERTHA . UNSPLASH.COM

Dear Friends,

Good morning and welcome to this chapter of relaxation skill. The much desired skill in extremely fast paced world!

> " *Relaxation is feeling of feeling lighter amidst heaviness of materialistic life's challenges . When you relax , you enjoy the sweet outcome of your achievements!*"

Normally clever students study for 3-4 hours daily to grasp the knowledge and polish their skill of comprehension, writing and preparing for exam. As the exam approaches, they need to put lots of efforts in practicing practice tests which make them aware about their skill of answering. However when you put lots of stress on your mind, you feel bored of doing same thing again and again and you need a kind of break for relaxation and doing nothing for some time.

We are pressed with competition and constant thinking to stay ahead in that limited elite club! What will happen if there is no competition, you can get admission with whatever marks you will get, there is no fixed curriculum time and you are allowed to study till you excel then there will be examination to look for your overall development. In such environment you will not feel any stress of performing but you will focus more and more on improving your skill to gain knowledge not answers. You will naturally think and develop the next stages of your research, inventions and efforts in various directions. This feeling give you relaxation. This is trick of entrepreneurship and good learning! Relaxation is nothing but carrying out your work without noting particular time limit.

Solve a paper with relax mind. Whatever you have read, understood and discussed with your peers will surely remember in exam and you can complete your answers with bright performance.

Similarly in business & entrepreneurship, your exam is with changing expectations of customer, performance of your products, reviews by your customers, the kind of innovations happened and changes in your market share. So whether you make a profit or not, always keep your mind relaxed. When your understanding of demand and supply becomes clear, you produce to fulfill demand and earn profit. A descent level of profit after some period make you feel relaxed and plan your future operations with more and more fineness ensuring accuracy and ease of your design by which you enhance your product quality , cut down costs and ensure profitability.

Creating a relaxed environment needs good understanding of human psychology. When you create interest in certain assignment , the day by day understanding of its link with various parts make you aware of the effects and you choose the best effect which act as success . When team of people club together and deliver to their potential, it creates success waves which makes atmosphere relaxed. This is about relaxed atmosphere at studies and at work.

What about relaxation at personal level. Friends, we know needs & wants have different meaning. Needs can be fulfilled but "want's "– Never! Its endless temptation! So if we need relaxation, we have to work out plan of minimum and maximum achievement by which we internally feel this much is sufficient and okay to lead a healthy, happy and handsome life! We have to avoid hungriness and to think about hunger!

Friends, family members and relatives are our best supporters and they like to associate with us for lifetime. So there is always a sigh of comfort that we are not alone! Facing challenges alone is difficult but when you believe in your full potential you are relaxed about its success. Friends, cricket is win by team of players while running and athletics are individual game. It's your ability to play both kind of game! In team game there are more hands for contribution while in individual game, you have to support yourself, you have to compete with yourself and you have to win over your last best performance in relaxed manner!

According to type of profession there are relaxation methods. A common man can relax with friendly chat while a scientist may need a path braking invention to feel relaxed. For a skilled doctor, a relieved patient from challenging health implication may feel relaxed while for an actor the inspiration taken from his film by people feel relaxed. Money all time cannot give relaxation; it's the happy response from your stakeholders which make you feel relaxed!

So the outline of relaxation is simple. Engage yourself in a different activity which can be hobby or any other skill. Body need some hours of rest while work provides you satisfaction of achievement to feel relax and sleep easily. A sound sleep is best indicator of an active and relaxed mind! Hope you like this chapter.

Let's take a pause here!

SKILL 52 : PARTYING & PARTICIPATING SKILL

PHOTO CREDIT : ERIC NOPANEN, UNSPLASH.COM

Good Morning Friends,

Welcome to this chapter – partying and participating skill. Let's know some socializing & informal networking!

> *"Parties are oldest way of success celebration, life event celebration or just for no reason. People have dire desire to meet each other, gel together and share best of life's achievement with dear ones!"*

Society is club of achievers, strugglers, educators, associates, partners, friends, relatives, family members, new bee's, veterans, scholars and common people. In such a large society, when we grow and work together, we form working level understanding and magic of co-working. We try different things, resolve problems, suggest solutions, experiment options, in all such cases we express our intent and emotion with each other. When our intent is clear and emotions are real, people associate with whole heart to support in every possible way. At the end of the day, we achieve our success or after some time we achieve our success. Perseverance is the thing which takes time to develop but it assures success. When such success is achieved, it is the result of cumulative efforts put up by everybody.

We celebrate such success in an altogether participative approach known as socializing through parties. Parties have fun element, good food, company of like-minded individuals and team with which you worked so far. Informal networking is great way of knowing each other through informal discussions, people chat with each other on various memories associated with their association , they discuss major contributions done by a specific player , the encourage each other to present their artistic skill, its completely fun fair .

Being participative means mixing with people. We generally tend to have different moods. Sometime we panic, sometime we remain silent, some time we work too much or sometimes we just do a mechanical work. But the mood of the party is always joyful, associative, it has easiest feel of team building.

> " The general start of the party is people gather together at a certain location representing the theme of the celebration. If its marriage party , the location can be garden hotels or party lawns. If its farewell party , the location can be most visited favorite places of the team. If it is success celebration party it can take place at beautiful outskirt of the city at a quiet, disturbance free place with enjoying party without disturbing each other. When number of friends unite together they may visit famous destinations to celebrate reunion . Why people dance or sing in party ? Answer is simple ! They create energy and improves mood of the party so as everybody feels charged up and become happy . The ultimate aim of partying is to become happy , develop relations and offer your insights if you come to know somebody is trying new stuffs in his career. Professional parties are more about socializing and maintaining decorum of the party . People are aware that fun needs to be fun and we are celebrating the success together so there should be general care about we are representing our brand in a publicly social gathering . This sense is very much important and event organizer or host generally share the basic details about party through a common standard informal suggestions !"

Some Basic Habits of Being Participative:

- Being participative means noting the chances of association.
- A meeting is happening and you are the one of the key team member, you have to give priority for this meeting by scheduling your work.
- In case a customer visits your office and at the same time you have to participate in one of the vendor summit, you have to take call on priority. If you are at senior position, you can make start with customer meeting with your core team, discuss the important matters and allow other team members to present at internal vendor summit, once you are comfortable with customer meeting, request some time to be part of their vendor summit and also share your views in meeting about achievements of last year with these team. This presents an absolutely transparent culture of performance, awareness for vendors about customer relationship management and example of flexibility for your team to work with two things at time with participative spirit.
- Talk with each other and spare time for informal discussions.
- Be attentive and respect time.
Friends, hope you like this chapter. Because of partying and participation, we know lot of things which are happening tangential to our life. Hope you enjoyed! Let's take a pause!

SKILL 53 : AGENCY INTERACTION SKILL

PHOTO CREDIT : CAMPAIGN CREATORS, UNSPLASH.COM

Dear Friends,

Good morning & welcome to new chapter- Agency Interaction Skill.

> *" Agencies supervise your system such as auditing agency, they provide you services such as calibration agency , they work for you such as third party inspection agency! Different purpose , different interactions! This understanding is must!*

As industrial revolution progressed, different forms of doing business are established. Earlier there was standard Employer- Employee relationship which deals with manufacturing of a part inside your premise by using your own technology and creating products with the use of available tools & tackles. Slowly, with rising demands, several big industries has observed, there is some part of work which can be done by other skilled people serving for us at a fair commercial value. This concept and logic has given rise to the concept of vendor ship. There are thousand small parts required for construction of a machine. Manufacturer decided to provide technological support in the form of firms drawing, manpower training, understanding of quality specifications and get work done by manpower and machines available at their vendor. This additional ecosystem proved successful and with passing days people got expertise and become vendors of a big brand.

This helped both. Manufacturer is getting exact replica of part they manufacture in organization with specification provided by him. Vendors got continuous work so as to supply their support services. From this work, few vendors got descent expertise and become designer and started developing their own product and became brand manufacturer by themselves. While becoming big they find some difficulty, hence they took help of some field expert and implemented their suggestions to grow their organization. These agencies could be manpower management agencies, reputed management consultant, statutory regulatory agencies, advertising and marketing agencies, channel partners and associates. This network of people coming together to serve society with their product worked for developing a brand and received its benefit once their brand got recognition and acceptance.

Interacting with all these agencies was a skill! When you are dealing with statutory & regulatory agencies you have to take care of details of regulation, trustworthy co-ordination with agency about kind of work you do in your premises and free access to them to visit your facility at any point of time without any prior permissions, resolution of technical or system related observations with regulatory protocol and adherence to their regulatory fees. The approval of statutory agencies for your work is equal to approval of people of that territory. Because statutory agencies represent people at large and you have to maintain trust with people.

Interacting with third party agencies which can visit your facility to represent for your customer requires detailed display of product progress with readiness and call to these parties when you are ready with your work. As they are customer representative and at the same time they are best marketer of your brand, you need to maintain a good transparency with your documents and processes to ensure their "remark & deviation free" field inspection reports. Feedback from such independent inspection agency creates brand value in market. Customers rely heavily on their reports. They have got independent existence.

Interacting with advertising and marketing agency is again a vital skill. You have to present your products, processes and manpower skill in presentable and appealing format. You create wonderful products and an AV create the first impression of your product by explaining your product in all together creative, entertaining and engaging way. Be it a promotional photo-shoot , design of poster, banners, hoardings or design of short movie , you have to keep your workplace professionally appealing !These agencies work act as the mirror of your workplace for customer as he can see your work on digital platform before booking an order with you. Rise of various e-commerce starts up is the best example of doing business with this way.

There are several other support service agencies like catering agency, security agency, calibration agency, labour contractors agency, transport agency, service support & maintenance agencies which provide support by which system get improved. In dealing with these agencies you have to keep formal and informal understanding of the way of dealing with them through terms and conditions of your contract. Agreements of these terms are one part while supply of actual service is another. A timely reported service increases chances of timely payments in system. Any delay in reporting creates delay in the system and because of which further activities also feels the impact. Hence time adherence is key with accepted terms of supply.

Friends, hope you liked this chapter. Let's take a pause here!

SKILL 54 : MARKET READING SKILL

PHOTO CREDIT : SONDER QUEST, UNSPLASH.COM

Dear Friends,

Good afternoon and welcome to this chapter – Market reading skill. Let's glance through it!

> *"Markets are best indicators of business offerings. You create, test and sale. The official destination of sales is market ! Market can be real or virtual !*
> *Financial transaction capacity of virtual platform make them recent favorite for most of the products!"*

Scenario 1:

Cell phones are become a necessity in just last 20 odd years. This technological marvel has made way of communication very very easy, fast and economical. The additional latest feature and market price has a clear relation. With addition of attractive feature and enhanced mode of communication, the prices are changed so far. We remember earlier mobile phones with press button small LCD screen; this was ranged between 5000-7000 INR. When this phone got replaced with smart phones with touch screen and enhanced internet connectivity it changed total market of electronics and telecommunication.

Data is become new fuel and because of internet connectivity phenomenal growth is achieved in digital marketing, social networking, and business expansion through e-commerce platforms. Market reading suddenly changed from Sensex closed and opened to No of views, downloads, like, comment, share. The basic philosophy of marketing a products which specifies when you like a product and when you like its manufacturer, you purchase.

Digital market reading is very very easy! We get complete analysis report of our offering through various creative dashboards to focus our attention, to craft out promotional strategy and to make us aware about real time sale. The transparency, trust and troubleshooting methods developed by e-platforms are great way to read market in easiest way!

Scenario 2:

A new innovation in the form of Electric Vehicle is about to hit markets soon. This innovation in case of proper success will become path breaking solution for auto industry. Traditional reliance on petrochemical products will considerably reduce which may reduce their demand and hence prices. Secondly, energy source of this vehicle is electric energy. With current available options of electric energy like hydral, wind , solar the fuel cost will be economically meet which will make launch of these product a big success.

As the technology will progress may be with advent of 5G spectrums, various on the go connectivity options may arise. So there will be new plans, new tools and new improved ways of doing things.

The prime mover sets the eco-system of their professional environment. When it was Automobile Boom, we have seen rise of thousand and million spare part manufacturers, their sales and supply network and required manpower and transport service provider. When IT boom happened, we observed exceptional rise of construction industry and enhanced level of urbanization. When it was green revolution , we observed phenomenal rise of crop production and same is for milk production revolution initiative ,So every new innovation with revolutionary capability changes market to a different level , it shifts choice and selection levels of customers , it gives opportunities for new player while few players has to think other options of survival.

Scenario 3:

Four groups of friends want to buy a property after their confirmation in a good MNC. They decided to book apartment in one big housing project accommodating 300 flats in 7 different wings. They went for site visit along with their family, observed the scheme and also reviewed nearest landmark and their current status. When they found whatever mentioned in their advertise is matching to reality they got convinced and started talk with builders delegates.

A price is told to them, to which they negotiated and because of group booking the builder offered them 15% discount on flats price. In this way because of group booking they benefited.

Had it done individually, they may have to pay bit higher amount depending on individual negotiation capability. Here, they were aware about this information of group booking discount to make sales of flat fast and easy and to make finance available to builder with initial payment. So this deal is beneficial to both. This is what entrepreneurship is all about!

Friends, hope you liked this chapter! Market reading skill is constant reading, observing & verifying the market trends to make beneficial decisions. Let's pause here! ✍

SKILL 55 : APPRAISAL MANAGEMENT SKILL

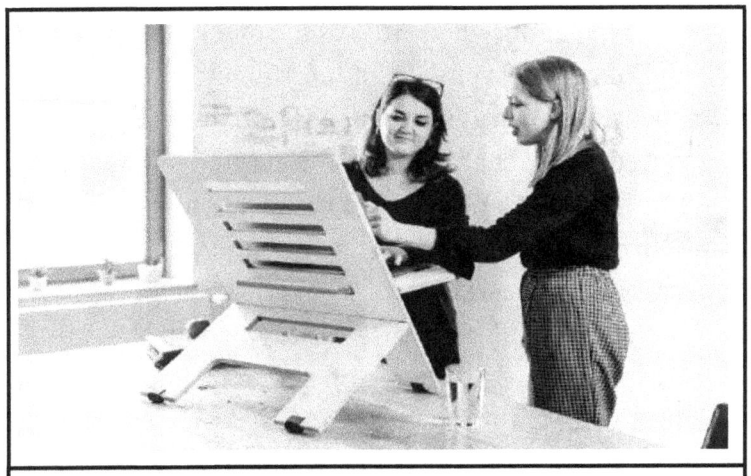

PHOTO CREDIT : STANDSOME WORKLIFESTYLE, UNSPLASH.COM

Dear Friends,

Good after noon & welcome to the new chapter – Appraisal management skill.

> *"Appraisals is systematic, generous and prosperous review of one's timely performance. Little laughter, detailed discussion and positive indications of expected salary increments and growth chances is what happens in a professional yet informal appraisals !"*

The informal appraisal scene:

1) The complete film making team works at several shoot locations in different environment , with variety of stuffs starting from action , dialogues , dance , suspense , thrill to present the character in best engaging way . It is the power of script that defines the overall plot of the drama, however accurate portrays of this drama with number of different characters individual & joint performance decides the success recipe and pairing chemistry. Let it be any situation and scenes, the best director know the true potential of his team and he allocate task which are best done by his team. Be it an action seen, he knows if I ask these two actors to fight together, they can fight in best entertaining way. If I want to show shades of love, then we can't think different pair than these two upcoming actors &actress. If I want to shoot a silent seen, then this actor is best at portraying silent, mature character efficiently. This casting is base of performance pattern and output of creativity knows as acting! Here produces will take care of finances but director has to look the actor or actress on whom I am counting, whether perform to need of the character and pace of the script. According to script changes, a seasoned actor improvises his creative mood patterns to go deeply into the roles and express those emotions in most convincing way! When this movie get created, the first hand impression of the

movie is received by the team with which we are working since last few days! When work is great, constant energy & happiness run in the unit that make environment lively, active and happy.

When this movie is shown in promos, we get first hand reactions about project and when he reaches screens we get immediate result of our work! Everybody has different choice and inclination. The view of directors, actor, critics and producers will be at one end and the view of general public will be at different end. General public will like to see their favorite stars; their character twists and theme that make them feel excited and entertained for three hours. If movie do this, it becomes a hit. Tickets are sold instantly and everywhere there is display of house full board. Then same movie perform differently at several global locations and stun box office! This fame, popularity and financial success make the project memorable. The support of people and Box office revenue are ultimate result of every film apart from liked story. When same actor or actress signs upcoming project, because of their brand value enhancement they can demand higher pridemoney for their work and perform to next best possible level and make movie a grand success. We know stars & superstars who have given consecutive hit movie to perform great at box office. Their charisma is what their appraisaldone by people.

The formal appraisal scene:

Here, story is real and script changes are real. We can have annual plan of business for a particular year but we face real time changes those occurs because of environment in which business is done. So every executive has to ensure the phenomenal display of their performance in reality to ensure their team works fine. Here you put all your creativity of design into product features and offering, you construct product as per specified codes and standard in a systematic manner and then sell it to market at a competitive price. The movie finishes in three hours but its impact or inspiration can remain for lifetime. When a sound technical product is created, the name of its creator is always appraised. This is the key of formal performance appraisals. When you work to provide result constantly, they are appreciated by team at respective forums. At the end of the year, it is just the systematic compilation and fact full presentation. Such appraisals starts with smile, discussed in detail and at the end we receive feedback which indicate a success in the form of possible salary rise or promotional opportunities. The skill is to go with all preparation. Admit errors happened and resolve any concern about performance improvement suggestion. This is what a good appraisal management is all about. Hope you liked it! Let's take a pause here!

SKILL 56 : INVESTMENT SKILL

PHOTO CREDIT : MARKUS SPISKE, UNSPLASH.COM

Good afternoon friends,

Welcome to new chapter – Investment skills!

Let's look into important aspects of this crucial skill!

Investment and return on investment are one of the important aspects of one's income and expenditure portfolio. Proper knowledge of various finance schemes gives timely benefit of your returns.

"We earn, we spend and we earn again and we spend again! When to Invest? How to invest? Why to invest? Where to invest? How much to invest? The string of questions comes to one's mind when we discuss about investments. Then comes the next thought of expected returns on the investment! What kind of returns it will be?

Increased sum? Added capacity? More and better safety? Additional income source? Tax benefits?
Mental satisfaction? Social contribution?

"Returns are achieved in variety of forms when investment is done in right,steady and futuristicdestination.
Courage , Financial discipline ,constant knowledge updating habit and a light heart which is balanced inprofit or loss out of the investment are good indicators of good investors!"

A big MNC start its operation in your country only looking after surety of returns on their valuable investments. The basic 5M's of management , a transparent ,time bound , accelerated strategy of growth , entry-stability-performance –exit strategy of organizations life cycle management , the national governance and their corporate affair policy , nearest market and basic infrastructure availability , all these factors are studied in details to invest in a big dollar deal ! This roadmap of strategic growth and expansion is well thought out by brands top executives and system support in the form of standard and specification make their path easy. Starting from entry into office to issuance of project completion certificate to customer, every activity is documented and it happens in same documented format at any location coming under that management system. So because of this system control, the brand respond constructively to changes occur in market and there is always a good command over production and profitability. Hence when my costs are under control, I am sure to decide optimum profit level. When I have enough money to expand my business, I take calculated risk and manage those risks time to time. This sets system in synchronization with its market at facility deliverers in steady profitable way as they stay in particular territory. So, as days pass, good returns starts following which gives desire feel of return on investment.

Tax liability is one of the prime concerns in establishing business. Availability of fundamental resources like water, electricity and land also plays important role in investing in a specific country. The federal laws and people's mindset for growth, science and productivity are other aspects that form investment decisions streamline. So when we think on this all round aspect, we come to final conclusion of investing in risk free productive and conducive environment! It assures satisfactory return on their investment!

In case of personal investment , the decisions to invest in safe destination is always on card , The traditional investment in Gold, Real Estate , Insurance Policies are well established now and people are looking to invest in various other recent options like Futures & Bonds, Stocks , Mutual Funds , Pension Funds , Health Plan ,systematic investment plans . By this entire means they are ensuring two things – reasonable return on their investments and tax concession in income tax liability.

Few Proven Investment Principles:

1) Start early, follow discipline and book profits before market goes sluggish.

2) Buy when organizations are new, study their vision and mission, overall infrastructure, manpower deployment, understanding of their product offering and invest in those shares.

3) For regular saving at least 10% amount ofincome has to save and invested in short, incremental saving plan.

4) Investment in education is best investment. Give free hand for this aspect. It starts giving return within twenty years to exponential percentage.

e.g. Investment in education up to Engineering may account to 20 Lakhs (YR 2021) , which can provide best job offer starting from 10 Lakhs to maybe 1 Crore if education done from reputed institute with descent industrial placements. Friends, hope you like this chapter, investment are always subject to market risk, but we have to enter into market! Let's pause here!

SKILL 57 : SHARING SKILL

PHOTO CREDIT : ELAINE CASAP, UNSPLASH.COM

Dear Friends,

Good Evening and welcome to this new chapter – sharing skill!

> *"Sharing is one of the most influential skills of a successful person. Sharing is basically providing support in any condition. It's the ability to stick around with your colleagues, friends, family & society. "*

"Share to care "is simple one liner that stands for importance of sharing. People work together, acquire knowledge and gain by sharing their knowledge, experience and difficulties to each other. It is the trick of sharing, which make people aware about a particular product or service about its features through various reviews. People create their opinion based on shared thoughts and their own experiences. When feeling and experience match with shared fact a permanent opinion is formed about a product or service which become identity of that product.

Basics of leadership and sharing have very keen association. There is informal hierarchy of sharing within team. Many strategies, decisions and plans are shared in different styles as per occurrence of events. This includes discussions related to new appointments, opinions about performance feedback, general plan of work or may be communication of outdoor travel plan. We share these things with each other in a trustworthy manner.

Advent of social media has created wonderful platform of sharing for people. Earlier people were away from each other with only traditional contact medium which can be mail or telephone. When mobile and internet is arrived, connectivity is improved to great extent and now minute to minute updates are available. Earlier for news, we have to wait for one day, but with dish TV and news channels, people find it easy to get visual output of days happening instantly, regularly and constantly. This made them aware!

Sharing has other aspect of informal association. You have a friendly relation with your colleague from last so many years. You are working so closely with each other. In one of the instance, you need leave and you share this thing with your colleague before discussing with your senior. He assures he will take care of your work based on priority of that day's work and then you get leave. You can avail leave as there is no strict compulsion but talking with your colleague in advance ensures sharing of work related communication and urgencies to make that day's work easy. This is how sharing helps to ease work pressures. When your colleague will also want to take leave, he will discuss with you and can avail leave in same fashion as you have done. This works both ways and it should be mutually beneficial to work in both ways.

Relations are built with sharing. When trust is created, you become reliable person and lots of good moments are shared. As per the year of practice in service when it is time to switch to managerial roles, your identity as a good approachable team member decided your success and your performance.

If from start of your career, if you have made friends, you have developed trustworthy relations and if you have taken people part seriously, there are no. of chances that you will be first choice for any leadership position based on your technical prudence and your personality. Sharing between senior and junior has always the feel of learning something great. You don't have to invest your time to reinvent the wheel; those experiences are fondly shared in a good senior-junior relationship.

Let's find out some of the important sharing aspect:

1) Sharing and reporting are two different concepts. Share with your friends about your challenges, in informal discussion we find easy solutions.

2) Meet regularly at various places, be it a coffee table, or a sport ground or shop floor corner. Discuss the status and your days plan. Make it habit to meet and discuss for about ten minutes with your reliable friend circle may be in college or office for informal sharing.

3) Trust is key, hence such communication is always honest and open.

4) Accept errors and mistakes. Stubborn stands always make sharing difficult.

5) People share some things which are highly secret; such things should be kept secret.

6) Interpersonal skill building starts with sharing. Having technical and managerial degree is one part while developing a performing engineer or manager personality is altogether different aspect. We need to create knowledgeable resources, associates and team member by networking, sharing and caring of mutual knowledge base to take joint decisions of your professional and personal relation. Tit for tat is rule of the game. But trust is proven equation! Hope you liked it! Let's pause here! ✍

SKILL 58: NIGHT WATCHMAN SKILL

PHOTO CREDIT : BEN MCLEOD, UNSPLASH.COM

Dear Friends,

Good Evening & welcome to new chapter of skill architect with one of the special skill of night watchman. Let's see what skillsets are must in this skill!

> " *Night watchman is a person who is not regular skill holder of a task but when responsibility comes on his shoulder to buy some time and stay firm in response to challenges , he delivers and perform !*"

It was fourth day of an interesting test match played between two strong teams on a wonderful cricket pitch. It was second innings and game of last inning was started ten overs before. In seventh over first wicket fallen and still ten overs game was balance. Who will come to bat? A regular player or a Night Watchman was the question. Captain of the team has sent the steadfast bowler of the team to look after this partnership. It was the game of ten more overs and if this partnership survives for ten overs, there were good chances of win on fifth day as only 240 run was the target. However because of the fifth days pitch, the ball was not bouncing and batting was become bit difficult. So the pair started their play and after over after over they keep playing and they keep wicket without loss. They do gather few runs and done fine to have sound position on fourth days play! On fifth day, same pair played up to teams 100 marks and continued up to 140 run at which the night watchman got his fifty and after two more over his wicket fall. The team needed 80 more runs and still eight wickets are balance. The regular batsman joined the new partnership and played well to win the match in next 20 overs with 8 wickets in hand! The partnership for second wicket by night watchman played the trick and helped regular batsman to stay relaxes till the time he was on wicket! On bowling part, in same match, he has taken 4 wickets in each inning. So his overall performance was fifty run and eight wickets, with 1 catch per inning. In shortly he owned that test match and announced as Man of the match because of his superb efforts to make team win!

Friends, this is what the skill of night watchman. Sometimes in business some situations occur where you have to represent yourself. Such situations have lots of challenges. The way of working are unknown, very few data is available, there is minimal support and you have to carry out any other teammates work in his absence or when he is gone for some urgent outdoor work travel. In such situation, you need to possess some skills which can take care of that situation. When you demonstrate this skill in front of team, if team like your way of working, they support you. In case your way of working is different, they will try to understand it and when they don't like your way of working even if it is as per rules and regulations, team will make situation more challenging to test your temperament. This happens and you have to possess the skill to tackle this situation. This is what the role of night watchman.

When you have sense of ownership, any responsibility become easy and you give your best to act like a star performer. With ownership, your performance crosses all the barriers and boundaries of performance and you always stay inspired and motivated. This motivation keeps you going long. Also when you are acting as a night watchman , there is always a senior who provide you necessary support however when the situation is so much challenging where senior also cannot help beyond a certain level , you have to pitch in and win that situation with your technical prudence , determination and tenacity to achieve great heights !

Preparation is key to success of night watchman's role. Always believe you have got great potential and with your passion you can do wonders! Always practice one of the great skills which are in demand. The time given to this skill determines your skill level. You have to invest time from your regular schedule, so always you have to stretch a bit to achieve those skills! When real situation comes, your preparation helps you to win over that time!

<u>Some basic tricks of a successful Night Watchman:</u>

1) Study the system in totality. Understand the job profiles, necessary knowledge level and growth opportunities.
2) Situations will come when regular people will not be available, at such moment, when you are available, people will ask to perform that task. As you are already prepared, you reach over there and delivers. This creates very good identity of your performance with increased trust level and thinking for suitable senior position in future.
3) As you visit new area, you learn to deal with new atmosphere, you create new working relations and understanding and this enhanced networking in fact spread your skills to new people. This is beneficial in lone term. So although some additional duties come, take it as future bonus approaching you to deliver for tomorrow. Hope you like this chapter. Let's pause here!

SKILL 59 : FUN AT WORK SKILL

PHOTO CREDIT : PRESCILLA DU PREEZ, UNSPLASH.COM

Dear Friends.

Good Morning and welcome to new exciting chapter – Fun at work skill! Let's have some fun here!

> *"When we enjoy our work every moment is a fun moment for us, this is because we like our work, we learn a lot from our work, we transfer youthful energy with our peers and it create fun at every successful attempts!"*

"Fun at work? "can be a good question which has many answers, it can be celebration of birthdays, it can be sharing delicious sweets with each other on achievement of milestones or having personal growth & joy, fun at work can be a light hearted joke happened over a communication and has made everybody laugh unconditionally, fun at work can be funful interaction with new joinees to make them comfortable with the environment. There are many ways which ensure everyone get feel of fun while doing their work.

Charged up work atmosphere is what the basic of a funful environment. We work with people and people have personalities. Somebody is special at errorless task execution, someone is expert of handling delicate situations, someone is fond of customer relationship management while someone like to share humorous jokes in lunch and breaks. All these activities creates conducive environment for fun!

It's the matter of first few months till we get aware about our daily tasks, our deliverables and our targets. Once we know the schedule and plan. We adhere to it. Sometime we have to join office early and make sure we are ready for that day expected level of good start. Sometimes we have to stretch for some time so that we can complete our work! When we practice this habit our work itself become fun for us. This is because we are totally devoted to our work! When we practice a particular task again and again, we become comfortable with its sequence and we get lots of fun when we do it! This is what enjoying our work.

When we are passionate about our work, we forget time limits. We take a problem in hand, analyze it thoroughly, break the problem into necessary solutions and then sort out the problem with every possible correct steps. This sequence of problem solving create fun and people love their work.

Ask a fitter, when he fits his set up with equal gap in between two joining parts, what kind of fun, pride and satisfaction he receives from his days work! Ask a new welder what kind of fun, satisfaction and joy he get when he observe a defect free joint after its radiography and ultrasonic test for a critical product which demands extremely high quality of weld joints. Ask a caster, what kind of joy he get when he meltdown the mettle into beautifully curved recess of mold and on solidification he get perfect porosity and shrinkage free casting. That joy is phenomenal!

You are following a customer for a new proposal and he has raised three –four queries to know more about your offering and you work out those concerns and present a descent presentation. Once he see your work, he gets happy and offer you the purchase order. This joy and fun is great always!

After a packed up eventful financial work the team decides to go on for outdoor activities and you become part of so many adventures activities and enjoy the trip to fullest, this joy is simply awesome and it helps to build team to a cohesive unit ,just like made for each other ! This creates fun!

Give and take is the law of the nature. When we take care of somebody, somebody will also take our care. This interpersonal understanding boosts trust and make environment happy and joyous all time . But what about when things are not happening as per plan or requirement ? It's the power of patience that work here . There are some tasks in which more time is required toget desired result . We have to wait for some time to achieve our results . When we build such patience with our team , we keep atmosphere calm and engaging. Thiscoolness make difficult things easy and as we approach to our successful path ,we starts feeling happy and this feeling creates fun for us!

When a job opening is posted , there is requirement of skills which can be technical as well as behavioral . Behavioral skill always take care of easy going attitude , go –getter approach and social animal hash tag . People love to work with such kind of team member who is talented ,humble and fun loving ! Such traits of personality goes long way in developing your leadership potential as you grow in your career.

Friends. Fun at work is about excellence at work , simplicity of process designs and easiness of its operations . When you practice pleasant ways of working by respecting delivery commitment and time of each other , things happens really quickly which makes environment happy and relaxing . Fun starts happening afterwards! Hope you like this chapter ! Let's pause here!

SKILL 60 : LEAVE IT OFF SKILL

PHOTO CREDIT : VITOLDA KLEIN, UNSPLASH.COM

Dear Friends,

Good Morning and welcome to new chapter –Leave it off skill! You may think what kind of skill this is ! But yes to lead a peaceful , happy and prosperous life you need to possess this skill of ' leave it off' for unwanted, unnecessary and unpleasant things happens in our life. Out life is full of opportunities and hopes . Hence even though we miss any opportunity , we get another chance to try our best!

> *"Thinking about past mistakes, failures and setback drain our mental and physical energy. A single no at the start of new things last in our memories till project success. A simple argument happened because of certain issue make things unpleasant. Sometimes we receives few setbacks which make us feel low, its natural but when we start leaving it off, we look at life with different perspectives! The skill of leave it off reduces junk of unnecessary thought and it provide you time to take actions! When you are absolutely clear in your thinking, your decisions can't go wrong. But is everything need to leave it off? No, we have to remember important crucks of the matter and leave it off rest! That what active listening and correct action is all about!"*

Let's see a story! It was a month end approaching and everybody was busy in putting their efforts to achieve targets. They were working on a new project and hence many new things were in place. People were trained to have seamless execution and also advised to display errors immediately. Being first job, everyone was curious about its test result and further success in the market. When the job was tested for intermediate testing, they observed low performance. When they analyzed the root cause, the observed a part of low capacity is fitted and hence it is not performing after its capacity is over whereas system is designed to perform for still higher result. With proper intervention , project manager given instruction to fit the assembly with right capacity of part . He has not argued nor scold anyone. They simply analyzed the root cause and took action . This is how they used the skill of leave it off to unnecessarily broadening the issue! In same job , when next phase of their assembly started , one of the assembly got fitment errors. The orientation got shifted by 1 degree which was causing matching problem with adjoining parts . Both part need a major rework and team was thinking how this is happened . Being a new product this was little setback but team decided to correct it with all due care. Supervisors applied their logic and prepared a fixture to ensure the alignment will never go wrong . They cut that assembly , reworked on it and then fitted on it properly . Here little resistance is shown by some people about kind of rework but since it was new job , the supervisor convinced everyone to carry out the rework and ensured a pre-check is added before proceeding for assembly of this joint. Here skill of supervisor worked to leave off unnecessary resistance which was logical but it should not be stretched beyond a certain level. They simply take a look of the things and corrected to go ahead !

In next step ,team got conscious and they planned to discuss that day's activity prior to its execution .They teamed up , discussed the sequence , allocated task and performed as per requirement . This helped to build job faster and everyone decided to work in same fashion for next jobs. This job was tested for final performance testing to which it shown very good result! At the end of product dispatch , team again sit together and discussed the learning of this project . They find out milestones and also discussed their future action plan on such new projects. They make a common understanding on which things to leave it off and which things to keep in right proportion to make execution easy and repeatable . This philosophy give them success.

Some Good gestures to leave it off things:

1) Nobody is perfect and we have to leave it off the imperfections to give them better chances of improvement.

2) Sometimes people tend to forge things.Sometimes they don't have the knowledge of necessary things yet they are assigned a task which make them to have few errors . In such a case a right and timely guidance help them to do better and achieve result. Here one has to leave it off the forgetting moments and has to rely on deep understanding of their assignment.

3) Sometimes failure in one project keep you down but when you leave the stress ,things can be planned in better way by working on their reasons of failure . Such gestures keep you on your mark to prepare you for GET-SET-GO!

Hope you liked this chapter. Let's pause here! ✐

SKILL 61 : THINK LIKE CEO SKILL

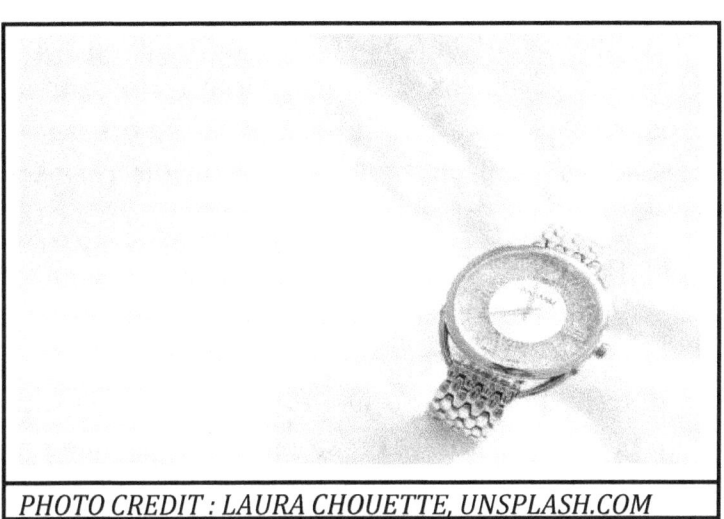

PHOTO CREDIT : LAURA CHOUETTE, UNSPLASH.COM

Dear Friends,

Good Morning and welcome to yet another new skill chapter – Think like CEO. Let's dive in!

> *" You are planning for next ten years of growth today and designing your approach to make it a reality ! This is what a CEO's thinking all about ! Superb vision, excellent ability to gain, maintains and sustains trust of public & board and executing the actions with flawless comfort!"*

A king par excellence Chatrapati Shivaji Maharaj, the scholars remember them as the brave heart inspiration and ultimate management guru has seen a dream of Swarajya – My kingdom in their early phase of life and gathered a 100% loyal and trustworthy team to make the dream a reality of freedom, law, justice and prosperity! Everyone has a respectable place in Swarajya. Everyone has a say in Swarajya. The valor and strength of Swarajya can be seen from the presence of majestic forts built and win by Raje in the rock-solid mountain lines of Sahyadri!

If we study "Swarajya" ideology thoroughly there was one vision to have our own land which is sovereign, developed and loved by everyone. This was the dream of a descent, powerful society of masses. To make this vision possible, there was systematic arrangement and planning done by the King with the help of their ministry who was expert of their field. People of swarajya were well aware about the affectionate nature of their king and they used to devote their wholehearted love and sincerity in developing swarajya with the duty they generally perform. The king used to expand the swarajya by acquiring forts with powerful battles and then establishing the saffron flag over their!

Off course there was struggle, issues of resources, availability of finances and most important environmental challenges to win fights in extreme condition where growth of science was very little. In such testing time, Raje used to follow their all senses to devise winning strategies. Strategies were completely unknown to their counterpart and this surprise element always kept their enemy under their control and authority.

Variety of challenges came across their extremely bust warrior's life. Which involved fights with mighty troop, battles of intellect and pride, negotiations of unexpected encounters and do or die type of efforts to establish the reality of swarajya ?

There was prudence guidance from Rajmata Jijau and all senior loyalist of swarajya . The Raje always discussed things with their beloved and trusted friends and allies. Whenever there used to big fight , they always gone there with their brave heart attitude and also told their trusted team to take care of swarajya in case some extreme adversities occur . Such was the devotion and such was the trust!

Battle , victory, treasure , authority , development of people and reasonable taxes to run the kingdom this is how swarajya grown with efforts of every brave soldiers, farmers and people at large .

Now moving to typical company culture which is best symbol of constant engagement with scientific discoveries and making real time applications for people at large ,The corporate CEO has always need to think ahead of time , may be ten to twenty years ahead. They need to be excellent student of economics and technical strength . Entry –stability- growth is the way of a successful business plans. Business plan reflect the beauty of CEO's vision . What is the best possible way of revenue generation, how business sum is to be created in market through successful IPO's and stock options , through knowledge about the sectors formal and informal way of working , fundamental ability to identify people strength and motivate them to perform better . Knowledge of basic aspect of legalities of business and how to keep business safe in all challenging situation is must know –how!

TO become a CEO you have to strive hard in initial days. It's the magic of your fundamental knowledge gathered at shop floor, design and marketing which show you path of design your product, create it and sell it at a reasonable profit in presence of your competition . You have to think about possibilities of several deals and make these deals successful. You have to form team of experts and professional and keep that team working to deliver result . When your one plant becomes successful you have to think for further expansion . You need to provide ownership and authority to people and at the same time you have to guide , coach and mentor them .

A good CEO always keep organization stable in turbulent environment, happy in challenging situations and attacking when market is bullish and favorable for growth . They have to ensure their decisions stand as model to work with satisfaction and in forward direction. Hope you liked this chapter!

Let's take a pause here!

SKILL 62 : THINK LIKE WORKMEN SKILL

PHOTO CREDIT : RICK HYNE, UNSPLASH.COM

Dear Friends,

Good afternoon and welcome to another chapter of the skill architect – Think like workmen skill ! Let's work on it!

> " In a confined space you have to enter a hollow shape and join two parts perfectly . The space available is enough to enter a very thin person . And you have developed and selected two such person to carry our such special joints!"

Friends, much time technical capability is proved by demonstrated performance at work. One simple line of 1 meter shown in the drawing for pipe or tube when created with the help of wire drawing process create several process errors which can be variation in ID & OD because of wall thickness change across total length, sagging of pipe in middle, ovality at face and process mark on skin, there may be possibility of joints not joined properly and there could be possibility that heat number may got incorrectly punched and created document error.

Friends, thinking like workmen means taking care of this possible error before actual loading is done.

"Before starting a work, every worker may be skilled, novice or veteran always does a first task of reading work allotment slip. Where I will invest my energy today and what are the challenges with that work. There are different work stations in a metals or manufacturing organization which involve various heating furnaces, machining centers, stores, tool cribs, open yards, set up and assembly stations, test bay or test enclosures, ground level work or work at height. He has to look all aspects of safety at work, performance at work and finally satisfaction because of that day's work. If work doesn't happens as per requirement, they feel so low and next day perform to best possible level!"

When we expect a seamless output from workers, we have to ensure whether we have planned the material required to complete the target, this is first checkpoint. If you are able to arrange material on time, then in next shift or same shift you can allocate your work pack to concern workmen and get work done.

When there are different machines and if one of the machine is not functioning properly and you have already put up requisition for its maintenance , then you have to think of the workload in totality to ensure work doesn't get stuck up because of possible stoppage of machine . Same thing is about availability of material handling equipment and devices.

Availability of crane is very very vital point in any shop floor. The design of shop floor speed depends on ease of travelling of its cranes. Because of crane and conveyor we can move in process material from one side to another, we can shift raw material from stock yard to actual work station. Apart from crane there are trolleys, bins, racks which are moved constantly as work progress. So you have to ensure your cranes and other equipment's are working fine.

Another challenge comes when you provide drawing to workmen. It is the only official medium of communication between you and them. Drawings need to be updated, neat and clean, easy to read with mention of latest revision. It is not expected that you carry those drawing with you but it is expected to keep all drawings easily accessible in their respective folder.

Tools and tackles and measuring instrument plays vital role is effectiveness at shop floor. Suppose if a pair of worker not getting a suitable hammer for their forging operation, they will ask somewhere else in house or will request for a new one. Till that time major time will be lost and you will not able to get output.

Availability of skilled workers is also a concern when dealing with critical loading condition. If a specific task is done by specific qualified person, you cannot allocate the work to other person. Hence this aspect also needs to take care to gain good quality work.

When there is good amount of dialogue with worker and supervisor, so many issues get resolved, but to think like workmen, you have to apply all practical concerns to ensure its seamless working. While thinking like workmen, you develop your planning, co-ordination, training, delegation skill to a highest level.

A new supervisor can take half an hour to decide the work pairing but a seasoned supervisor does the same task in mere five –ten minute. The reason is they know every fine details of every workman and there is fond association and emotional attachment which do their work.

Friends, think like a workmen to ensure you think practicalities of job. Rest care is taken by workmen. When a pair of workmen observes total readiness, they ensure they deliver it best! ✍

SKILL 63 : THINK LIKE ENGINEER SKILL

PHOTO CREDIT : THIS IS ENGG., UNSPLASH.COM

Good Morning Dear Friends,

Welcome to yet another skill chapter – Think like an Engineer skill! Let's design & implement this skill!

> " *Creativity and analytical ability is the basis of sound engineering knowledge. Attention to details and root cause analysis is the true identity of a progressive engineer. Engineers are technical problem resolver, if they can't resolve a problem, they can't eat!*"

- When it comes about setting more things in less space, think like an engineer. How many things can be put backward; which are not used regularly! How many things need to keep forward; which are used regularly! How many things can be put outside active work place so as to bring them inside whenever required! How many things need to keep strictly in Loctite cupboard to avoid their mis use! What should be the size of various compartments so that it will host maximum no of items and less blank space remain available! How the display of things to be arranged to facilitate their easy loading and unloading! How to order things by just observing minimum stock level meter line! If you are using available space to its best possible allocation, you are almost thinking like an Engineer!

- When you are forced to face unexpected event always think like an engineer. Adversities and challenges are normal things of an engineer's work life. First thing to such instance is book your emotional response to this situation. Because when problem occurs, first thing happens is irritation and anxiety in mind! Engineers think quietly, decide quickly and act rapidly to resolve the matter easily!

- You don't have enough resources to buy the things you need. Learn & develop those skills for which you are buying those things. It's the matter of journey of first few products. Once you create your identity in market, things starts happening quickly in your favor. In early training of a particular engineering stream, engineer knows how to join

things, how to tight things and how to arrange things in systematic order and sequence.
- Multitasking and time management is important skill Engineers possess. Actually the person who practice multitasking and time management are no less than engineers. Engineers work on multiple things same time, its start- wait –finish kind of sequence. Suppose you are carrying out three tasks at same time. You first analyze the task that will take more time, then next and then task which will take least time. You work out their stages and general time requirement. Then you start with their steps and allow time to finish, meanwhile you focus on different task and arrange things which are required to start the work, then you moved to third task. People are working on tasks and they report you status. You observe the accuracy of their work and suggest improvement measures if required. This way you manages multiple work same time.
- The journey of noting interrelation between system elements and setting a favorable connection and avoiding or blocking unfavorable connection is normal design principles used by engineers. You observe and think about design of a pressure pump. There is arrangement of various valves to control flow. When you are pumping water from ground and supplying to somewhere else, you are fixing a strong pipeline connection, system of gate or globe valve to allow water to start or stop, you put a foot valve to take care of low levels of water and signal accordingly. You also put a non-return valve to

avoid back flow of water. When so much deep thinking is done you design a particular pump system according to its usage requirement. Lot of study is done by scholars and the work is available in the form of standards and specification. You study those specifications and arrange material and manufacture. You test its performance, improve on observations and market it! This is what a product launch activity generally practiced. This thinking is proven thinking and it has resolved so many difficulties of people. Think in this way!

- Observe the risk and think in a positive direction always. This is what engineers do! Every work has some risks associated with its execution. Engineer observes the behaviors of risk and plans their response. When it is about repairing a circuit, the first thing need to do is cut the supply of electricity and then move ahead with safety precautions. In a supply off condition, you open the circuit, note the status of part and replace or repair it! Then again you start the supply and observe the result. When things work, you complete your work! Masters always prefer safety as they have to serve more customers for long time!

Friends, ability to think, act and apply are fundamental ability of human being. You don't need to be a formal engineering degree to have this skill. What matters is your never ending desire to resolve the problems; this is what engineers practice every day! Hope you liked this chapter! Let's pause here! ✍

SKILL 64 : SPRITUAL SKILL

PHOTO CREDIT : JOSHUA EARLE, UNSPLASH.COM

Dear Friends,

Good morning and welcome to yet another skill chapter – spiritual skill!

> *"Physical, mental and spiritual! These are the three levels of human interaction with this universe!*
> *Although I am not an expert of all, but I am a good student of these three life paths of constant learning and uplifting your mind, body, soul regularly!"*

Childhood is the stage of life where we play, learn and grow. At this age we indirectly observe and practice the social and spiritual customs when we are living in a peaceful and prosperous society. Parents and teacher tell us the age old philosophies of good human to human interactions and to make it clear that although we have power but there is supreme power in the universe which drives this universe. Some may call this power as Almighty, some may call as nature or some may call as a pioneer of divinity, who protects us!

As we progress in our life, we become more curious about understanding the details of spirituality and subject called as soul. It is assumed as per Vedic philosophy that every human being and living being has made up of mind, body and soul! Soul is the supreme and soulless body means there is no living presence! The philosophy to understand the soul is spirituality.

Progress is sign of hunger to do better. In a material world, people strive hard to earn their living. It is practiced that whatever we earn through our hard work must be used for our livelihood and buying our needs of material comfort. This can be a good house, good car and other offerings such as jewelry, bank balance and other investments.

The basic career life of everyone gets busy with doing their assigned duties, achieving targets and receiving money for their efforts. From this money various EMI are paid for loan reimbursements and day by day we become free from our borrowings and start feeling like an owner of particular belonging. The feeling of ownership is awesome and it gives us a separate identity, enhanced status and feeling of pride! To enhance this feeling, people tend to achieve more and more and this new feeling generate various enemy's for peaceful living which are called as **kama (extreme physical desire) , krodha(anger) , lobh(possessiveness) , mad(unnecessary pride) , moha(dire need of getting something) , matsar (jealousy)!**

These six enemies of soul occupy our mind and make us believe in material aspect completely. People tend to have different levels of material gain, when they are satisfied, they tend to earn more and when they are not fulfilled they feel anxious, stressed and restless.

As per Vedic philosophy every human being has three kind of nature or behavioral characteristics which are **satva (pure & gentle), raja (royal), and tama**

(Angry). So to live a satisfied, prosperous life the reasons which create anxiety, stress, excessive desire has to be controlled by practicing techniques of self-talk, need analysis and meditative practices to keep mind cool and calm.

We have five sensory organs and our mind is their supreme controller .When we control our mind with the help of meditation, we feel relaxed and we work with good intent and do good deeds. This approach reduces errors and keeps us energetic and happy throughout the day!

An edge reaches in life when we are free from our responsibility and we are almost retired. This is the edge where we find our self physically weak, mentally low. This is the time to increase spiritual practice and immerse yourself into deep yoga and meditation. This relaxes your mind and you retain life energy.

Although everyone knows the lifecycle events, yet everyone is running behind steep targets and monetary achievements. Where this will end? Nowhere! The greed is endless however need does have sure end. If I earn lakh rupees and if in fifty thousand I manage my expenses, slowly and steadily, I am going to save for my future and hence will lead a happy life. Then it is my call to really go to any extent for the sake of money. When this understanding is cleared in mind and we take our actions accordingly, we feel light and happy.

Comparison and competition make you restless. However if you have unique skill, you can become safe breadwinner for your family. This is what spiritual thinking guides to every sincere disciple. Acquire supreme knowledge, earn your living with hard work and pride and be in touch with almighty with the help of eternal chanting to understand the real meaning of life which is to serve for other and forget your sorrows. Service of mankind is service to almighty. That's it! This is spiritual skill is all about!

Friends, hope you liked this chapter.

Let's pause here! ✍

SKILL 65 : STORY TELLING SKILL

PHOTO CREDIT : ADAM WINGER, UNSPLASH.COM

Dear Friends,

Good Evening and welcome to yet another skill chapter – Story telling skill! Remember, this skill is important part of marketing your product or service!

> " *Stories are important, they tell facts and myths increative and expressive ways. They touch heart andmake you believe in your concept!*"

In business you interact with number of stakeholders. This can be your customers, vendors, team members and general public in organizations social events! At every moment, you need to present your views, your examples and your decisions to people listening to your presentation.

Stories are entertaining way of providing factual information in an engaging manner. Suppose there is new customer visit where delegates are coming to your office for first time. Now here it is your duty to provide information about your work location, the general growth story of organization, milestones and rewards. This best way to have direct interaction in front of team working with you to showcase your potential, strength and market presence.

Corporate movies is become a norm now-a-days and hence story telling of your organization become so much important. We are using video communication for most of our business purpose and hence sharing your expertise through such video presentation is widely accepted and practiced. These videos can be shared on social sites and hence your product reaches large no of masses at same time.

Every corporate story has a humble beginning starting from a low investment, less resources and high aspiration initiative. This is the power of aspirations which convert low investment to enhanced market capital, fewer resources to qualified high end manpower and your increased motivation to achieve more and more. This complete journey you have to show through your corporate videos. Once you written theme of your movie, next step is provide visuals of your facility which involve your credentials, specialty of brand, kind of customers you serve, display of critical machines which you use for regular working, skill of your manpower and their online working demonstration. This is followed by your social initiative and other achievements which sets you apart from other competitors and connect to most of your customer.

Storytelling is basically about expressing a situation with people present over there! How things happened? What is their logical linking? How you managed that situation? Who helped you? How serious was the situation? Which tool helped you to survive through that situation?

If the story is related with a product success, then what was the status before launch of product? How things changed with this product launch? Which are the benefits of your product in comparison to other product? What is the overall lifetime of product and how this is useful in considerable time frame? This type of introduction is part of a good product storytelling.

In a typical service related story telling, you have to introduce about your service in short and you have to contact people who have used your service or product. You have to take their interviews through well designed questionnaire and record their true responses. You need to keep responses real and true. This creates genuine impression of your product. When you compile best interviews, your movie is ready and you can show it to your customers and viewers at large which can become your customer later!

Editing is important part of storytelling. Lots of time when people are not seasoned about facing video camera there are chances that the presentation may look dull and boring. To make people express their true feeling you have to train them about facing the camera. You have to show them their first recording and their expression and you have to take second shot for right expressions. In editing you have to cut expressions in which there are fumble or in between stoppage or voice clarity issue. In editing, you ensure a presentable recording.

Upgrades are normal part of storytelling and you incorporate newest methods of graphical element in your story telling videos observing latest trends. The voice modulation also plays important part and you have to ensure a noise free voice for good audio quality.

Always keep complete silence before speaking on camera to capture surround noise level which can be removed in editing sequence later .Noise reduction technique is one of the best practices to receive a studio quality sound! Tell your story with pauses, laughter's, and fact checks, examples and people experience and in the end ask people about their feedback to prepare for next presentation. Hope you liked it! Let's pause! ✍

SKILL 66 : PRACTICING SKILL

PHOTO CREDIT : SAM MOQADAM, UNSPLASH.COM

Dear Friends,

Good Morning and welcome to yet another skill chapter – Practicing Skill!

> *"Practice makes man work hard for their success.*
> *Practice let you know the details in deep.*
> *Improvement happens with regular practice. The efforts done and time invested in practice provide you necessary confidence of winning!"*

In schools , we learn mathematics. Mathematics is a very very funful, exciting and important subject if we understand its formulae correctly. If we remember the steps to resolve sums and if we practice it often. There are number tables; basic math's which goes on increasing up to theorems of calculus and geometry. Mathematics is all about establishing a universal relation with things and principles observed in the universe. Such studies are going on from ancient time and now computing skills are reached up to artificial intelligence & machine learning logic building!

Practice is vital in achieving required proficiency in mathematics. It involves understanding the relation between variables, remembering constant values which are derived out of empirical studies; we have to note units of conversion and then the total list of numbers for which we have to do calculations to note the span of our work.

When we become perfect in maths, our answers tally with answers shown in model answer sheet. When we know the math's formulae, at any place we can solve problems. Whatever data is presented to us and whatever may be the situation in which data values are observed , once we note the mathematical approach to given data value , we apply relative formula and work out solution of that problem.

We know there are four mathematical actions which are addition, subtraction, multiplication and division. All further mathematics revolves around same equations and actions. In different theories, we observe different logical approaches. If a trigonometric equation when we are given an equation and asked to tally with other equation, we put up formulas in between and get the answer and show there are two approached to same problem. This is the fun of learning maths. You come to know different path of your success.

Compared to all other subject, mathematics give you guarantee of 100% marks if you resolve all problems correctly. This surety make you work harder and practice the formulae till they become by heart. In this system of practice you go on solving same or similar puzzles with different practical situations. Because of which you can find practical relationship of mathematics with the rest of the world.

Now when we think of business and relation of practice we can easily find out the equation, more efforts we put into business, more is our growth. Understanding customer inclination and preparing product that fulfill their requirement is the basic mathematics every businessman wants to know. Secondly setting right value of your product and keeping your profit margin in tact assures you desired comfort level which comes after careful study of market and your products marketable features. People and their buying behavior are your challenges with every transaction and the quality of your product is the formula to resolve that equation. Quality of your product is improved with repeat production, reduced errors and enhanced skill of your workforce. To achieve this skill level you train your manpower and engage them in challenging tasks. More time they spend with their work, more facts they understand about their work and become master of that trade. Mastery is nothing but knowing complete cause-effect cycle of system under practice.

Few Practice Principles:

- Practice needs regularity, patience and perseverance along with thoughtful actions!
- In practice same thing is done again and again with improved responses to same situation.
- As we go on practicing, we set a feel of things, their occurrence and when our response needs to start exactly in dealing with that situation. For example in cricket if you want to play spin attack Comfortably, you need to know how to come forward and hit out of the ground and at the same time you have to practice skill of returning before wicket keeper stumped down! To achieve this skill, you need to practice in net for several hours with different combination of spin attack which can be leg spin, off spin and types of deliveries.
- The Momentum achieved after practice needs to be improved by regular touch. A little time invested goes long way to become an expert. Hope you liked this chapter. Read the success stories of people and you will see extent of practice supporting it!

    Let's pause here! ✍

SKILL 67 : ISSUE UNDERSTANDING SKILL

PHOTO CREDIT : LEON, UNSPLASH.COM

Dear Friends,

Good morning and warm welcome to this new chapter – issue understanding skill!

> " *Some simple situations when overlooked or not acted at right time by right individuals become an issue later wards. Constant communication and follow up is key to resolve issues!*"

Mega factories have millions of transaction's happening every year. Systems are so robust that there is specific time allotted for every activity with thoughtful studies. Any break in standard operation is liable for immediate corrective action by which piling of work is avoided and continuity is sought in all endeavors.

There are executives, managers, workmen, leaders , board and various expert associated with mega factories to constantly analyze market and take necessary steps to maintain the growth . So issues at such factories are always negligible and if they happen regularly the major action is taken by leadership.

Investors and trade analyst also play vital role in investing and disinvesting in particular organization. Their participations in particular sector decide their interest level and hopes from that sector all according to demand analysis.

But how much kind of issues arises and what are their remedies? Issues can be technical or behavioral. Issues can be financial or social. Issues can be permanent or temporary. Issues can be related to individual or team of professionals. Issues can be related with quality or quantity. Issues can be allotting more time for operation or for reducing given time of operation as more parts to be produced from same method. The segregation of issue is key to decide action plan to counterbalance.

Technical issues are resolved by approaching right knowledge basket. It's very very simple to resolve technical issues when we know the exact root cause of its occurrence. To resolve behavioral issues constant dialogue is key. People behave in certain fashion to keep them safe from certain things which they don't like. Such things can be always find our and corrective actions can be taken. For example, because of repeat rejections, many people feels, quality managers are there for rejection, but is this true? If quality manager or any of the team member associated with quality is run away from their duty norms and if started accepting inferior quality material, that material will fail in future or may not give required performance. In such cases they might face strict interrogation from their customers and they will always feel discomfortable is explaining the reasons. Even after the reasons are told, customer will not stop till he gets his resolution. This is why every attempt is to be done to make your product reliable, affordable and respectable. This is why quality managers and executives need to be sharp and focused about the process steps, deviations and restriction measures.

Financial and social issues require money capital and human capital. Banks are always open to support business with proper validation. Suppliers are always ready to support a business on their credit. Vendors can wait for their payment for some time if your earlier payment transactions are regular. Social issues involve the effect of your product or service on society. If you follow regulation, you majorly avoid social issues. Because you are creating a safe product, getting it reviewed by concern authority who is people's representative and then selling it to market. Now if customer really needs it, they will surely buy it at any cost. You have to ensure your products are safe and easy to use!

Issues of permanent nature are always discussed till its mutual agreement and approval. Temporary issues are resolved with quick action. The burden associated with an issue reduces it speed of decision making. There are various opinions from team which make it difficult to have common understanding. This is the reason why issues become larger than they actually are!

Quality and quantity issues are dealt by optimizing process design and adding capacity to your workplace. When you expect enhanced performance from same machine, because of time restriction, you cannot complete all task and in speed up action, quality get reduced. Hence we need to add other machine to enhance capacity and maintain quality. Issues of more time or less time are always related to observation of unnecessary time wastages in system while working practically. They are dealt with time studies and their suggested measures! Issue understanding is the first step to resolve issue with right action & decision.

Friends, hope you like this chapter! Let's pause here! ✍

SKILL 68 : KNOWLEDGE BUILDING SKILL

PHOTO CREDIT : CLAY BANKS, UNSPLASH.COM

Dear Friends,

Good morning and welcome to yet another chapter of skills, this time – knowledge building skill!

> " Learning is a constant process. Knowledge is supreme . Without knowledge , you cannot take correct decisions. Incorrect decision leads to losses hampering your growth prospectus. Learn everydayslowly, steadily, firmly!"

Knowledge building means adding latest information, data and images to your memory. This content will always guide you to observe at actual situation with reference to memory data and take correct decision. Same as a computer! But in case of human decisions there are number of factors which are time dependent. There is element of choice and element of satisfaction behind every decision. The decision taken with proper knowledge yields good result while decision taken with insufficient information lead to stuck somewhere middle of the game!

> *" Knowledge is key driver of human psyche . There are number of branches in which specific knowledge is given with proper curriculum consisting of theories and practical's. Apart from formal syllabus , there are reference book and on line study material with which knowledge can be acquired. Discussion with experienced team members adds great value to your knowledge domain . Cross functional interaction adds great facts to your practice . It is not necessary to read complete book alone, practical life is about learning through sharing .*
>
> *Attending major seminars, participating and various exhibitions and trainings , involvement in quiz and competitions help you add knowledge ! Knowledge is biggest intellectual property one can have !*

Lets look at proper knowledge building programme:

- Post SSC, plan your professional interest and start moving in that direction through formal qualification. Now-a –days , preparation are staring from playgroup level as more and more parents become aware about benefits of education and competition of this field. Systematic coaching programs are also available from standard seventh or eighth which prepares a strong foundation to build those skills.
- Ask questions to your teacher or instructor. Teachers and instructor has long years of experience in dealing with professional terms and they have interacted with so many student which help them understand potential of every student.
- Always approach a subject with tremendous curiosity. Curiosity will make your world. It will attract you towards different subject matter and encourage you to dive deep.
- As we learn from practical experiences, we never forget that experience. An hour of practice in an industrial environment is equal to reading 100 pages of that subject's book! But then why books are required. The answer is book can be written only after working in such environment for number of years to know how things work.

Book is extended form of experiences, lessons, facts, tables, graphs which enhance our comprehension. Read good books in company of

good friends!
- When we work we get tired. To become fresh again we play sport or hang out here and there. During travel or sport we come across several different personalities and observe their responses to particular scene. This is also a certain type of knowledge building. With study of body language you can easily decide the right response to make better relations with peoplearound you!
- Currently lot of online courses is available through number of online platforms. Television and internet has number of channels which support academic channels. With the availability of academic video, now you can gain knowledge as per your own comfort level.
- Certification and licenses make you aware about latest addition in a particular knowledge domain. The certificates which have limited validity ensure you have constant touch with your work along with necessary knowledge. To keep your license live, you have to work in that field continuously. Hence you need to go through constant up gradation of your system.
- Foreign tours are great ways of building knowledge. Every country has different development. With such travels we come across new methods of socio-economic happenings.

Friends, hope you liked this chapter!

Let's pause here! ✍

SKILL 69 : ACTION TAKING SKILL

PHOTO CREDIT : PIETRO MATTIA, UNSPLASH.COM

Dear Friends,

Good morning and welcome to new skill chapter – Action taking skill! Let's see into the details.

> *"Actions represent logical expressions of work. Actions can be right or wrong depending on the accuracy of decisions which depends on analysis of situation which depends upon data available to take such decisions!"*

You are a quality engineer in a manufacturing set up and facing following situations:

Situation 1 : A set up has got wrong orientation and it needs rectification. What actions will you take to bring the things to normalcy?

Action:

- Check with respect to drawing and as per views shown in the sectional details.
- Discuss with the fitters along with supervisors, the cause of error and stage of the error.
- A rework or set up correction require part to be removed from incorrect position, do proper cleaning of earlier work and refit to required orientation.
- Check with respect to applicable drawings and suggest proceeding further.

Situation 2: A set up has got wrong orientation and it needs rectification. The error is noted after welding of these parts!

What actions will you take to bring the things to normalcy?

Action:

- Check with respect to applicable drawing and check list details, how this is happened.
- If this is miss out in inspection, accept it and carry out an improvement plan with filing NCR.

If the set up welded in hurry before communication of result, ask to feel NCR
- Seek permission for rework from authorities with the help of respective NCR.
- First remove respective joint from joined portion safely by cutting with gas cutting torch.
- Grind the burnt edges and do the joint preparation for re-set up.
- Refit the joint with necessary weld gap arrangement.
- Get it checked and approved.
- Weld it to required weld size.

Situation 3: A set up has got wrong orientation and it needs rectification. The error is done by your supplier and part is received in finished good condition.

What actions will you take to bring the things to normalcy?

- Call respective buyer immediately and provide him necessary vendor code and part details to convey the rework message to vendor.
- Suggest vendor to come up with checklist and drawing used at the time of manufacturing of this job.
- Ask vendor reasons of error and guide them for necessary improvement in their system.
- If authority allows, send the part for rework at vendor end with outside work pass, carry out the

rectification as per drawing and bring the part inside by checking with respect to outward gate pass.
- Suggests to carry out in-house rework ifpermissions are not given. In that case debit respective cost of rework to vendor and take vendors conscience for same.
- Check the rework from your end and pass the stage.

Verification, analysis, documentary evidences are necessary steps of taking right action. Once things are accepted, they can be worked out with the help of applicable policies and instructions. Every action has equal and opposite reaction. Hence it is necessary that if there are any strict actions all the facts should be verified and actions should be taken in good spirit.

To avoid repetition of serious errors, proper training should be given to every team member and stages to be monitored by observing its process carefully. It is grossly proven that whenever there is careless ness or knowledge gap, things go wrong. So while building this skill of action taking, you have to remain courageous, strong and clear in your decision. Such decisions are fixed and irrevocable. Hence actions are understood to be serious concern for everybody.

Hope you like this chapter. Actions defined speed of decision making. A delayed action create enlargement of small problem and give rise to serious problems.

Let's pause here with a note of timely action. ✍

SKILL 70 : CONSTRUCTIVE DELEGATION SKILL

PHOTO CREDIT : MD. DURAN, UNSPLASH.COM

Dear Friends,

Good morning and welcome to new skill chapter – constructive delegation skill . Let's see how things move when we do accurate delegation .

> *" Delegation is an art of allocating some part of work to team working with you with proper guidance, monitoring and correcting errors if any!"*

Let's see some general examples of Constructive Delegation :

Situation 1 : You are a quality engineer and you have responsibility to offer stage of manufacturing to external inspector. The stage need to review radiography reports, destructive testing reports, your dimension check report, visual inspection report, all documents , permission stamps and final drawing of product.

How you will lead & delegate the task to ensure remark free acceptance from external inspectors.

Leading & Delegating :

- As you are working in manufacturing shop , you are aware about the status of job and where job can reach within next two days . Accordingly when you are asked to offer the job for inspection , you will cross check its status to understand its readiness. Once you are sure with readiness you will decide to move ahead!
- First you will take concurrence from your shop shift engineers about completion of balance work before inspectors arrives.
- You will check and collect reports of completed testing . For in process testing you will wait for reports. For not ready testing , you will confirm the time required to get test samples and their test plan . On satisfactory internal testing you will review reports.

- Then you will verify the dimensions and visual check points. If you are satisfied with status, you will prepare report of acceptance. If there are rework points a few locations, you will guide about how to carry out the rework.
- In your internal document review, you will ensure every report is available with all its necessary details. You will ensure all serial numbers are correct and necessary supporting documents are available.
- When you are thoroughly satisfied with overall status of the product, you will notify your external authority about status of stage and their availability for inspection.
- With common understanding you will fix a date and will report to concern stakeholders. Now this part was about leading the situation.
- In delegation, you will ensure with destructive and non-destructive team to complete the task as per test indent and you will review the report and sign for same.
- In dimension check, you will take help of your colleague and confirm dimension along with him. For visual inspection, you will jointly see the part and discuss rework points. If there are any arguments, you will explain the requirement of rework with the help of applicable standard.
- For call administration, you will talk with your office security and admin function to look after hospitality arrangement.

- To fix your meeting on day of visit, you will reserve the meeting room to ensure a fix time slot. You will allow other meeting on that day upto a certain time.
- On the day of visit, you will receive all report, review from your side and stamp it.
- You will check for arrangement and communicate the time of arrival.
- Once external inspector is arrived, you will greet them and confirm the plan of the day. With their informal approval of plan, you will proceed to respective workstation.
- You will observe inspection and assist to clear improvement points if recommended by the external inspector.
- You will get your report reviewed and will send a copy for inspectors reference.
- On satisfactory completion of visit you will ensure readiness at canteen and have your meal together.
- Later you will sign off security pass with thanking external inspector for their presence and guidance. Here, you have lead as well as delegated some of the task to other & cross functional team members. The end result was success of a team work in constructive way!

Friends, hope you liked this chapter.

Let's pause here!

SKILL 71 : SURPRISE ELEMENT SKILL

PHOTO CREDIT :BEN WHITE , UNSPLASH.COM

Dear Friends,

Good afternoon and welcome to another skill chapter – The surprise element skill . Let's see in detail .

> " Surprise has power to energize the atmosphere immediately ! These skills are less used skills and can be your hobby or special expertise or can be very very special activity which is difficult for other and easy foryou! "

How Surprise Skill Works? :

Situation 1 :

You are an Engineer and works with a reputed organization . Its annual day and you are asked to showcase your creative skill . You think and tell organizers to present your anchoring skill . Organizers take your audition and they get stunned by observing you style of presentation , way of capturing details and overall presence of your personality when viewed on stage.

On the day of function , you present your skills with sophisticated professional style and now not only organizers but everyone out there become amazed with your superb performance . Now whenever there is such type of functions , you are cordially invited to anchor the party . So this skill has added a different glow to your personality .

Situation 2 :

You are visiting an outdoor site with your three other colleague . You visit the site and observe there is a boat club available to try your hands with water . Your friends are not aware about your skill and you show them how boat is run in water . You ask them to sit with you and you make superb ferry over there . Your friends feel happy and surprised and insist to train them also. Out of three , one of the friends learns it quickly and on return way , he drives the boat . Not to forget , you all are present there with safety jacket & all know swimming.

Situation 3:

On a project site you are gone to check status of the project . Number of parts is lying over there and it became very very difficult to make space for your parts . Your job is to check the status and prepare a report for presentation to your seniors. To make this task easy , your take two people for your support and ask them to show part no with respect to packing list of offering . Meanwhile you ask them to clean part external surface to have clear feel of surface condition . People help you and in three hours you can verify status of 100 small parts . You are observing identification , noting random dimensions along with their supporting dimensional report and approving inspected parts . During inspection , one of the parts is received incorrectly with respect to reports provided . You note it and communicate to concern people . Concern team member verify the feedback and feel surprised to observe your observation and detailing skill . This error has avoided a major rework which could have happened ! Not only this , you seek permission for its replacement with your courteous talk with customer. Customer asks few questions about your system control and how this misses out is happened . You explain them with practical example chances of miss-out and your methods to full proof it. You also tell them person inspecting the item is a skilled inspector and such kind of things never happened from his side . You also present your commitment to quality aspect and you will never give chance to complain about quality issue. Customer accepts your sincerity & diplomatic skill of discussion in the adverse and difficult to convince situation . You manage replacement within two days and ensure part is available before it actually required for fitment. This make everyone happy and they feel surprised about your relation management skill with internal as well as external environment.

Friends surprise skill has a certain pattern , let's discuss:

- You cherish your hobbies and with constant investment you excel in that hobby . When presented in regular environment , this becomes surprise for everyone.
- There are many adventures and sports. In our free time , we practice it and become skillful . In the organization there are sport events. When you participate and win ,it becomes a surprise and it adds to your new identity.
- When working in a cross functional team , we learn other functions skill also . When you switch over for departments, these habits make you fluent with those functions responsibilities. People feel surprised about your flexibility and this flexibility leads to generate bigger potential to become a big player.

Friends, hope you like this chapter.

Let's pause here!

SKILL 72 : ANALYSIS SKILL

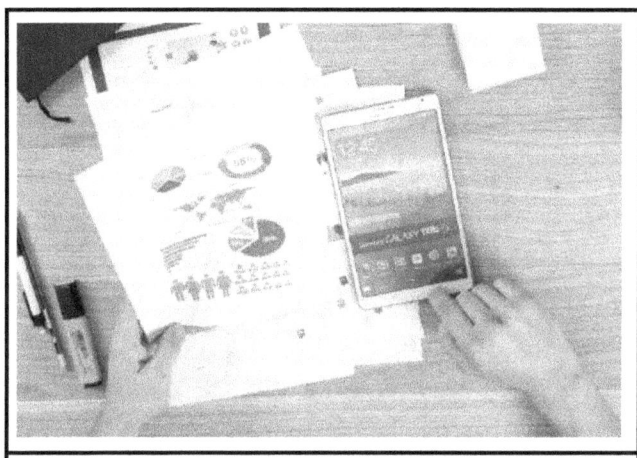

PHOTO CREDIT : FIRMBEE, UNSPLASH.COM

Dear Friends,

Good afternoon and welcome to this new skill chapter – Analysis Skill !

> *"Analysis is step by step understanding of factors associated with process, situations or happenings! A cricket match has detailed analysis of player's performance with respect to their counterpart which helps to identify the end result of match to great extent!"*

- Y = mx +C is a general slope equation.
- $(a-b)^2 = a^2 -2ab + b^2$ is school level mathematical equation.
- % x= % y / %t x 100 is basic equation for percentage to calculate possible percentage value with respect to actual value to determine span of specific data in a typical pie chart.

Friends, analytical ability is exceptional ability of a person who believes in data centric decision making and hence improved accuracy of their decisions. Analysis is always done to measure properties of a product or service quality of a particular offering to number of customer. We all are aware about video sharing platforms. These platforms very systematically analyze the performance of your videos based on number of users , your reach , specific watch time , specific watch hours and hence overall viewership of your videos. This data help you to excel on your performance and deliver better presentations next time.

When you have to carry out analysis ,we majorly use office products those can processes your data to show mathematical relationship of your data. All the functions are available in these software's which present you bird eye view and detailed view of your data to focus on particular aspects. More practice you do with these software's, you work with ease and present data in easiest form. A live cricket match analysis help to understand the inclination of match, performance and form of a player , their previous track record, their performance on particular location . This data help viewers to enjoy the match with not only four and sixes but also show the latest ways of data presentation. Looking upon graphics of the game , at any point of time we can observe the start to finish happening of game on single graph .

Business analytics always make you comfortable with market understanding, forecasting and trends and your strategies to effectively enter into a particular market at favorable time . Entry into market is very very important decision and this makes you perform with great speed . In a booming market there is high demand for your product. Once you enter in that market and earn your customers and serve them better ,you start receiving more orders and thus establish yourself into market.

In a cricket match , the analysis of a bowler involve how many overs he has bowled , how many runs he has given , how many wickets he has taken and how many maiden overs he has bowled. Same observations are done for all bowlers to have a descent comparison. At the end of the game, we compare the performance of batsman with respect to number of balls they played, runs earned , no of fours and sixes and result of the match . When the performance of winning side is compared , the best one who is major contributor for team's success is selected as man of the match . So if someone question why the particular person is selected as man of the match , there is factual analysis of their performance for that match . When every match is analyzed for a series, the top performer for series bags man of the series award. When number of series is played by a player in his tenure , it becomes his track record which indicates number of wins or losses when he played a certain special knock. When this track record is maintained for long time, such players are rewarded with prestigious civilian awards . So when overall life's performance is observed , we get instant record of our achievement and challenges because of this timely compilation of data. When number of players is analyzed for their record , it reflects sport culture of that country which help to plan sport event for particular year and by which you commercialize your respective business through these sports. So because of analysis and its scientific views you are able to make major capital investment decisions.

Performance of any business is analyzed through its balance sheet. Balance sheet indicate you your assets & liabilities along with your turnover , break up of your expenses and overheads, depreciation and taxation concerns, profit before and after tax and dividend paid to your shareholders on particular face value of your shares. So to make investment in any share market ,you take help of analysis of its balance sheet . A healthy balance sheet records profits and has less or nil loan liability. Friends, hope you liked this chapter .

Let's pause here! ✍

SKILL 73 : SALARY MANAGEMENET SKILL

PHOTO CREDIT : ROLAND SAMUEL, UNSPLASH.COM

Dear Friends,

Good Evening and welcome to new chapter of skills – Salary management skill, one of the favorite chapter of everyone, isn't it?

> *" Salary is remuneration and recognition of efforts. Salary management is about saving descent amount of money after your monthly expenditures !"*

You join as trainee engineer and get the first hand feel of your first salary. This money is very very special. Not only for you but also for everyone who dreamed for you, worked hard for your success and who constantly loved and supported you. It is the journey of six years starting from standard eleventh to standard sixteenth. In these six years, you study with a target in mind. Either to set own enterprise or to become an employee of a big corporate house where you will get paid handsome sum , you will be having excellent job profile and all learning of an excellent place to work and nice people to work with.

But not everyone is employable not they get good job at first instance. People have to struggle for good job, good references and good recommendations. They work hard, very hard to achieve a position of respect and success. In these initial years of struggle, you get opportunity to work with small capacity enterprises where you have to do lot of activities. These activities give you sufficient practical knowledge and understanding of overall working.

As days pass and month end approaches, you receive your salary which may be in few thousands. You may be single or maybe supporting your family as single bread winner if you are from humble background. In such situation, you find it very comfortable to receive this hard earned salary as your normal expenses sufficiently managed from this salary. It is moment of pride for your all family members!

After two years, when you get enough experience, you either discuss with your superiors or they by themselves raise your salary to satisfactory extent. Now you can do more expenses or you can decide to take up higher studies if you have saved some amount from your salary if you can. In these two years you can save a small sum and invest in systematic investment plan. You can keep your installments comfortable to you which you can save easily. This is just to make you habitual to use your salary carefully.

In case you wish to marry then most of the time youngsters prefer to book their own home or they modify their old home. This is because; home is symbol of stability, status and prosperity. Here your salary management skill starts working. Most of the flat cost heavily and they consume approximately 7 years' salary if you are receiving at least 5 lakhs per annum in 2021, with considering cost of one BHK as 35 Lakhs. If your salary after joining organization is less than five lakhs, you have to immediately think for other options by which you can improve your take home salary. This can be done by doing extra training courses to add skills and certifications. If you are updating your job profile on career sites, you may receive an interview call for suitable position. If you pass interview with good performance you can ask for good rise. Which can be become 20-40% depending on organization, location and current market condition. So if with this salary you cross 5 Lakhs marks in first two years of joining, you can instantly approach your bank and apply for your home loan. As a prudent negotiator, you have to put lot of energy in searching a good, quiet home in peaceful society. Here with your negotiation skill you can set your budget by getting at least 1 lakh of discount. That much skill you have to acquire before approaching a builder. Once you finalize your home, you get married and you start a family. Expenses increases and if you are single bread winner, it creates little stress on managing expenses. Youngster now-a-days prefer to have working partner for same reason. You both work for your aspirations and manage the show with help, support and guidance of your parents and in laws. These people act as torch bearer for you as they have superb experience of how a house is run!

After 4-5 years when you are ready for kid, your expense goes on increasing at constant rate. However by this time you both have nice experience and you get handsome rise so as you can fulfill your ambition of dream car. You approach for car loan with your earlier loans repayment track record. Depending on your market credit, you get qualified amount for your loan amount.

In ten years when you are free with car loan and home loan, rest is saving for your middle & senior age try for entrepreneurial assignment if you wish, take care of your parents and enjoy the upbringing of your kids with beautiful holiday trips. At work, you get senior positions and paid handsome salaries. This is what life Up to superannuation after which you get your funds. Hope you like this! Lets pause!

SKILL 74 : LEARN & EARN SKILL

PHOTO CREDIT : ANGII NURIAMAN, UNSPLASH.COM

Dear Friends,

Good Evening and welcome to new chapter of skills – Learn & Earn skill!

> *"Learning is important phase of life while earning is mean with which life is lived ! Its great habit to start your earning early in the life when you are learning !It gives you academic and practical awareness about how money is earned in society!"*

Friends , penny penny make a rupee or a dollar! This is what importance of money in life. Earning money is not so easy .Unless you have upmarket qualifications, personality and skills, earning money always become a distant dream. We are diverse people and everyone is not acquainted with comforts of life. Some struggling friends has to do struggles for basic survival, they have to arrange for their tuition fees from hard work by their parents. Taking education like Engineering is always a herculean task for such families. Still talent is one thing which does not allow settling quietly in life. Your talent motivates you to cross all limits of your capacity to become winner of life!

If you are residing in village then there are fewer earning opportunity while you learning. Basically expenses are less in villages and Taluka places. In villages you can get part time work related to farm activities or you can work in your own farm by implementing advanced methods of farming or by setting up a small cowshed with the help of which you can sell milk to city and earn descent profit. Processing of agri products is a major activity in villages. You can always try your hands at various seasons to make work available for you.

If you are living in Taluka place, there are some shops and offices where helping hand is required above certain age. As child labour is prohibited, you have to engage in suitable opportunity like taking tuitions of kids or setting your small vegetable stall in market just to have feel of market and to get little bit profit from that activity. Now –a –days because of information technology and other movement of internet video streaming is become a good option along with various software courses by which you can improve your computer skills to develop yourself as good IT student. Here you can develop new mobile apps, organize your studies, can have social networking and can receive new work.

When you are living in city, right from selling newspaper to selling industrial products, you have lots of job opportunities. The markets are bigger and you can get part time work adhering to child labour age concern and earn few bucks. You can provide easy services in which there is no hard work and some clerical or data entry support is required.

In learning through science projects and art projects we get feel of how to prepare these equipment and artwork. In e-commerce age, you can always display your products on leading sites and start your small business adhering to age approval concern of 18 years.

We always give priority to learning for 25 years as this age is very much receptive and age of our all-round academic and social development. So we must schedule our studies to make learning a great fun and yet saving some time to earn few bucks. Although you earn 100 Rs per day by working 1 or 2 hour, you will save 3000 Rs by month end which will take care of your study material and future saving.

Some Easy Tricks to manage both Learning & Earning:

- Manage your time systematically. If you attend your school or college regularly, your study will get complete over there only.
- Newspapers give advertise for part time work. Visit such places and request for work. If you found suitable, you will be given work.
- Do your duties carefully and report your work.
- Save money earned for your future education by opening a bank account. If you saved it elsewhere its fine but ensure to not spend for unnecessary expenses.
- Build a robust body to learn and earn.
- Develop good relation with people working over there and learn professional skills by assisting them in their work.
- Two years is nominal time to get easy with working environment. Ensure regularity andpunctuality.
- There is good quality reading material available for school and college going student. Use that material. This is your development age in which you know various earning options.
- Stay positive and help each other. Things moves really simple for people exercising descent co-operation and enthusiasm.

Friends, hope you liked this chapter. Take care of your hardly earn money and money will take your care! Let's pause here! ✍

SKILL 75 : TARGET SETTING SKILL

PHOTO CREDIT :AUSTIN DISTEL . UNSPLASH.COM

Dear Friends,

Good Evening and welcome to yet another skill chapter -Target setting skill!

> " Target setting is giving justice to your potential. Target setting is about systematic planning of your work in hand to finish it within time and with desired quality . Target setting is indicator of your performance limit!"

Target Setting for students:

- Student life is full of energy, enthusiasm and learning new things at rapid pace. More you learn in less time determines your grasping capacity which is supported by your ability to memories whatever you grasped for longer time to ensure you understood the concept clearly.
- Students need to practice target setting to qualify for various entrance exams and criteria fulfillment for various interviews.
- Screening is first hurdle which they need to cross with the help of qualification marks.
- Hence student has to study exam pattern, curriculum and model question-answer papers. Later they have to plan their time of answering questions. This time management acts as crucial.
- More questions you practice, more aspects you can understand. With every error or mistake you come to know about right answers. In this way you remember right answer not only by reading it right and accurate but also by noting right answer when you answer it wrongly.
- Good writing practice is yet another skill for successful target setting and its achievement.
- The time of study is always an important aspect of achieving your target. When you are feeling fresh, your energy levels are higher which ensure complete dedication and enthusiasm with which you achieve your targets and achieve results safely.

Target setting for professionals:

- Professional target setting is about achieving desired result in allocated time frame. Generally professional have quarterly, semester and annual target limits. Sometime same is minimized to daily target achievement.
- Before start of work, they have to analyze availability of required resources.
- After analysis they need to start the work with correct completion approach.
- These approaches are provided by quality plan of stage and their sequence.
- Many a time to make their work variety of tools and tackles are provided. Every professional has to use these work simplifiers to make their work easy and fast.
- Safety at work is an important concern. When there are safe working conditions, people work fast and comfortably.
- At every completed stage it is necessary to ensure correctness of work. When things are right at their first instance, further operations get a push and completes fast!
- When you need to enhance your performance, you always start early, plan early and monitor your work steps to ensure error free work.
- Habit is best supporter. When you successfully attempt work completion with smart tricks, it become your second identity of target achiever.
- Target setting is fun! Enjoy it often!

Target setting for leaders & managers:

- Actual analysis of strength, weakness, opportunity and threat is done before setting any target.
- Definition of target itself is the identity of a strong leader. Achieving 10 Crore in year and achieving 15 crore in year with same set up is what the difference of leadership. Strong leaders contribute more with their wonderful technical & business expertise.
- You develop your people to best possible extent. You have to ensure the adhere to individual performance expectation to achieve your target.
- You discuss, coach and mentor them on continuous basis. This helps you to achieve descent momentum over challenges faced by your team.
- You control, improve and facilitate internal and external environment. This gives timely idea about target completion.
- Any changes or set backs are momentarily affect you. You immediately devise your action plan to support your next actions.
- You network with great people. These people act as best supporter to meet your targets. In the end you enjoy with these friends to boost your chances of further success and continuous link of success. Friends, target setting is an art. Hope you liked this chapter.

    Let's pause here! ✍

VOLUME CLOSURE

Friends,

Hope you like the skill chapter and overall book structure. We have tried to keep the most informative content interesting and simple yet effective as far as practical skill building is concerned.

As we have committed in preface of the book, we have spread this book into three volumes each comprising 75 skills!

The skill wise distribution will be like follow

1) Volume 1 – Skill 1 to 75
2) Volume 2 – Skill 76 to 150
3) Volume 3- Skill 151- 225

Herewith we confirm the completion of first volume. The chapter numbers of second volume will start from 76 while chapter numbers of volume 3 will follow from skill 151. Kindly take note of same for further reference.

The intent of this break up is portability and ease of reading! Thanks!

REFERENCES

This book is written on the basis of 13 years of professional, managerial experience & 37 years of life experience. Which involve experience of study, travel, adventure, profession, competition and leisure activities!

The primary aim of this book is to provide easy access of practical skills and job knowledge to every newcomer, interested individual and general practitioner of Engineering & management domain.

All the efforts are done to present the subject adhering to organizations copyrights and other intellectual concerns.

We herewith express examples given in this book are not to be quoted and they are mentioned for simplification of concept.

For any kind of concern, we are available at

ppt.inspection3@gmail.com

Phone: 91-9970173983.

Thank You!

Have a nice time!

NOTES

NOTES

NOTES

www.ingramcontent.com/pod-product-compliance
Lightning Source LLC
Chambersburg PA
CBHW071445220526
45472CB00003B/674